The Timber Bubble That Burst

THE TIMBER BUBBLE THAT BURST

*Government Policy
and the Bailout of 1984*

Joe P. Mattey

New York   Oxford
OXFORD UNIVERSITY PRESS
1990

Oxford University Press

Oxford   New York   Toronto
Delhi   Bombay   Calcutta   Madras   Karachi
Petaling Jaya   Singapore   Hong Kong   Tokyo
Nairobi   Dar es Salaam   Cape Town
Melbourne   Auckland

and associated companies in
Berlin   Ibadan

Copyright © 1990 by Oxford University Press, Inc.

Published by Oxford University Press, Inc.,
200 Madison Avenue, New York, New York 10016

Oxford is a registered trademark of Oxford University Press

Library of Congress Cataloging-in-Publication Data
Mattey, Joe P.
The timber bubble that burst:government policy and the bailout of 1984 /
by Joe Mattey.
p.   cm.
Revision of thesis (Ph.D.)—University of California, Berkeley, 1988.
Includes bibliographical references.   ISBN 0-19-506275-2
1. Lumber trade—Northwest, Pacific.
2. Lumber trade—Government policy—United States.
I. Title.
HD9757.A19M38   1990
338.1'7498'09795—dc20   89-70954

9 8 7 6 5 4 3 2 1

Printed in the United States of America
on acid-free paper

Preface

This book examines one particular microcosm in which the government plays a large role, the market for federal timber in the Coastal Pacific Northwest. When read literally, the book is about an unusual episode in economic history, a bubblelike movement in federal timber prices that led to a massive buyout of federal timber contracts by the forest products industry. When read as a parable, the book provides more general insights into the effects of government policy on private business decisions in the United States.

The book considers two competing paradigms of thought about the relationship between government policy and private sector behavior:

1. People are very sophisticated about macroeconomic policy, and there are no microeconomic distortions to prevent achievement of an efficient, competitive equilibrium.
2. People are essentially blind to macroeconomic policy developments but very sophisticated about how to take advantage of microeconomic distortions.

The book argues that the second paradigm is closer to the truth.

Chapter 1 introduces the reader to the market for federal timber and the timber contract crisis. Chapter 2 tries to explain timber price movements in the context of the first paradigm—timber buyers are responsive to macroeconomic policy developments, but in the early 1980s the macroeconomic environment changed so radically that they were fooled temporarily. The third chapter tries to explain timber price movements in the context of the second paradigm— timber buyers are responsive to microeconomic distortions created by federal timber sale policies, and in the early 1980s these distortions encouraged the buyers to take great risks on timber contracts.

Judging whether timber prices were more affected by micro-economic policy than by macroeconomic policy would be easier if the beliefs of timber buyers were observable; chapter 4 discusses the psychology of the federal timber market, explaining how misconceptions about economic relations helped timber buyers rationalize their decision to take great risks on timber contracts. The concluding chapter reviews how timber sale policies have been reformed in the aftermath of the bailout and proposes further reforms.

While this book should be of most interest to academic economists who are concerned with macroeconomics or forest economics, it also is written for nonprofessional readers who are interested in the timber contract buyout. The book is based on my doctoral dissertation in economics at the University of California, Berkeley. The dissertation contains some technical material that has been omitted from the book; any reader interested in formal modeling of timber contract price determination is encouraged to consult the dissertation (Mattey, 1988). Chapter 2 of the book uses an econometric model to quantify rational response to changes in the macroeconomic environment. To keep each chapter accessible to the nonprofessional reader, I have described this model in an appendix.

Many people and institutions have provided invaluable support. I am particularly grateful to George Akerlof, who inspired me to look at economic behavior in novel ways. George, Dick Meese, Jim Pierce, and Dan Sichel are among the many people who made helpful comments on earlier versions of the manuscript. Forest Service staff at the Pacific Northwest office in Portland, Pacific Southwest office in San Francisco, and central office in Washington, D.C., have been extremely helpful. Financial support for graduate study in economics from an Edwin, Frederick, and Walter Beinecke Memorial Scholarship and an Alfred P. Sloan Foundation dissertation fellowship is gratefully acknowledged.

This book is dedicated to my wife, Shaley. Her affection for the Pacific Northwest sparked my interest in this subject, and her willingness to listen to the tale of the timber contract crisis helped me complete the book.

Washington, D.C.
December 1989   J.P.M.

Contents

The Timber Bubble That Burst

1

Introduction

The federal government has a large impact on the economy of the Pacific Northwest through macroeconomic policies and timber sale policies. In recent years, many members of the forest products industry have questioned the federal government's ability to perform effectively either of its economic policy roles—beneficent timber baron or macroeconomic policymaker. Criticism of the federal government reached a high point in 1982, when timber buyers found themselves holding contracts for national forest timber that obligated them to pay roughly five times more than the current value of the timber. They had acquired the contracts at public auctions conducted by the Bureau of Land Management (BLM) and the United States Forest Service (USFS). These agencies were castigated for letting the industry bid timber prices up to nonviable levels, while macroeconomic policymakers were criticized for engineering a recession that drove the demand for wood products to unexpected lows. Members of the forest products industry claimed that the timber contracts would have been profitable under the macroeconomic policies in place at the time the overpriced contracts were written.

This book explores both of these charges. A careful examination of the evidence suggests that federal timber sales procedures were the primary cause of the fiasco. In retrospect, however, it appears unlikely that the calamity could have been avoided by the adoption of a more predictable macroeconomic policy.

The Bubble That Burst

As shown in Figure 1-1, USFS douglas-fir timber contract prices increased explosively in the late 1970s and declined precipitously in

3

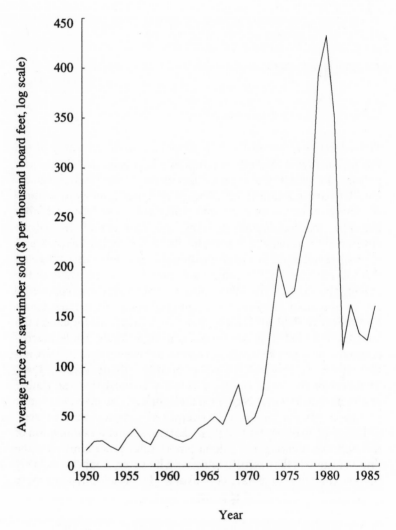

FIGURE 1-1. Douglas-fir timber price on national forests.

the early 1980s. Timber prices grew and grew, and then burst, like an overinflated bubble.

The series plotted in Figure 1-1 is the average price of douglas-fir timber on long-term contracts for cutting rights in forests in the western portions of Oregon and Washington. The USFS demarcates this area as the west side of Region 6. The region also is known as the Coastal Region because it lies on the Pacific Coast side of the Cascade Mountain range, and it is known as the Douglas-Fir Region because douglas-fir is a predominant species of tree in this area.[1]

During the 1970s and early 1980s, the most common form of contract in the Coastal Region specified that the purchaser would harvest the timber by a given date and would pay for the timber when it was cut. An oral- or a sealed-bid auction was held to determine to whom the contract was awarded. The highest bidder was deemed to be that person who agreed to the highest estimated payment amount, with the estimated payment amount being determined by applying the species-specific payment rates set during the auction to the Forest Service's estimate of timber volumes in the sale. The actual payment amount was determined by these same rates applied to the actual volume of timber removed from the forest. The series plotted in Figure 1-1 is the average bid rate for douglas-fir timber on newly issued contracts in the Coastal region for the years 1950 to 1985.

In one sense, the calamity in the Coastal region developed in late 1979. At this time, quarterly timber contract prices were continuing to increase at a rate greater than 20 percent per annum, but lumber prices were beginning to fall sharply as the demand for wood for housing construction substantially softened. During the first quarter of 1980, the average timber contract price peaked at roughly $300 per thousand board feet lumber tally (MBF, LT). Throughout the remainder of 1980–81, prices on newly issued timber contracts remained extremely high, even though no rebound in housing construction was in sight.

By the fall of 1981, it was apparent that widespread defaults on federal timber contracts were imminent, and in October the Forest Service liberalized its contract extension policy, allowing contract holders to extend contracts for two years upon payment of interest on the total contract liability. The western timber industry began to mount a substantial lobbying effort, asking Congress to pass legislation to nullify overpriced timber contracts.

In 1982, many of the timber contracts that had been written in late 1979 and in 1980 were due to expire. On average, when the costs of converting timber into lumber were taken into account, timber in 1982 was worth less than $60/MBF, LT. The difference between what timber contract buyers had agreed to pay for federal timber and what they could profitably afford to pay for the timber was roughly $250/MBF, LT. This difference was so large that many timber buyers faced insolvency.

The contract extensions that the USFS granted in 1981 allowed timber buyers to delay harvests. This delay severely disrupted local community services because local governments depended on the sharing of federal timber revenues as a primary source of income. Citizens in timber-dependent communities increasingly joined the clamor for contract modification as they struggled to keep their schools open, police personnel on the beat, and other community services intact.

The Bailout

The Ninety-seventh Congress considered several bills to allow termination of timber contracts. In August 1982, public hearings were held on the merits of contract modification, and many timber buyers made a pilgrimage to Washington, D.C., to plead for relief. None of the bills made it through the Ninety-seventh Congress, partially because Senator Howard Metzenbaum of Ohio strongly objected to any legislation that provided significant benefits to the few large forest products firms that were still quite well capitalized.

The coastal timber industry had better luck with the Ninety-eighth Congress, but only after protracted and heated debate. Further hearings on contract modification were held in April and May 1983. When neither of the two bailout bills being considered made it out of committee by the end of July, President Reagan authorized the extension of timber contracts for up to five years; interest payments on the contracts were waived. Congress ultimately passed the Federal Timber Contract Payment Modifications Act of 1984 (FTCPMA), and this act was signed into law by President Reagan in October 1984.[2]

The FTCPMA also is known as the "Timber Contract Buyout," because it permitted qualifying timber contract holders to be absolved of their liabilities upon payment of a specified buyout charge. This book calls the FTCPMA the "bailout of 1984" because the act saved many forest products firms from insolvency.

The FTCPMA was designed to benefit firms that faced insolvency from timber contract losses more than firms that were still well capitalized. Contract holders were permitted to buy out up to 55 percent of the timber volume on contracts issued before January 1, 1982, but no more than 200 million board feet. The buyout charges depended on the extent of the purchaser's losses: If the losses exceeded the firm's net book worth, a minimum buyout rate of $10/MBF applied. Otherwise, the buyout rate varied with buyout volume and the ratio of the purchaser's loss to net book worth.

In the nation as a whole, purchasers returned about $9\frac{3}{4}$ billion board feet (BBF) of timber to the BLM and the USFS by paying about $170 million in buyout charges.[3] About two-thirds of the returned timber was in USFS Region 6.

In Region 6, 190 firms filed buyout applications.[4] These firms held slightly more than 19 BBF of timber on contracts issued before January 1, 1982. The contract price on the eligible timber on average exceeded the appraised value of the timber by about $250/MBF, LS, giving the group an aggregate overbid of almost $5 billion. The FTCPMA provided a way for these 190 firms to buy out of about 8.5 BBF of timber at a cost of roughly $135 million. Almost three-fourths of the firms that bought out of Region 6 sales were eligible for the minimum buyout rate on all the returned sales, indicating that roughly three-fourths of the firms would have been insolvent if forced to pay default charges on the basis of appraised values.

As with any historical event, there was no sole cause of the overbidding episode. The limited extant research on the circumstances that led to the bailout has focused on how various contractual features affected the decision to delay harvest (Rucker and Leffler, 1986). In the aftermath of the bailout, the Forest Service has modified its timber sales procedures in ways that reduce the purchasing firms' exposure to product price fluctuations (Muraoka and Watson, 1986), but many of the basic preconditions for the episode still exist.

An Overview of the Book

This book investigates two claims:

1. That an unexpected change in macroeconomic policy created a gargantuan forecast error that drove a wedge between timber contract prices and ex post facto timber contract values.
2. That alternative timber sale procedures would have prevented the escalation of timber prices.

It examines the role of macroeconomic and timber sale policies in the timber contract overbidding.

Undoubtedly, macroeconomic policy was a source of instability in the timber market. However, a review of the evidence suggests that timber bid prices were unresponsive to available information about economic conditions, and that the error in predicting the macroeconomic environment does not explain much of the timber overbidding. In the early 1980s, the federal government pursued a disinflationary, deficit-prone macroeconomic policy that depressed residential construction and the demand for forest products. Timber buyers who were fully rational in the sense that they forecast as if they knew the way the economy worked but failed to anticipate this course of macroeconomic policy would have lowered their bids on timber-forward contracts when they learned about the chosen policy. However, as shown in Chapter 2, timber prices remained high long after it became clear that the macroeconomic environment was sluggish and the lumber market was depressed.

Federal timber sales policies also were a source of instability in the timber market. Part of the escalation in timber prices can be attributed to a perceived shift in the path of public timber supply. The industry had overinvested in plant and equipment relative to the realized path of timber supply. Under the existing timber sales procedures, the cost of financing USFS timber purchases was insensitive to the risk that the purchaser would default. As shown in Chapter 3, firms that pursued the corresponding incentive to gamble on timber contracts instead of disinvesting of their plant and equipment were responsible for much of the increase in timber prices.

Overly optimistic expectations about future timber values also were a source of instability in the timber market. These optimistic expectations appear to have been fostered by cognitive dissonance—

timber buyers preferred expectations that were consonant with the belief that they would survive the shakeout in the industry. They interpreted available economic information in a way that rationalized their choice to gamble on the contracts. As explained in Chapter 4, forecasts produced by the USFS facilitated the adoption of false, but preferred, beliefs.

The concluding chapter discusses reforms introduced in the market for federal timber in the aftermath of the bailout. Many of the problems that contributed to the timber contract fiasco still exist, and further reforms are proposed.[5]

2

Victims of a Macroeconomic Policy Shift?

Prima Facie Evidence

There is a substantial amount of prima facie evidence that timber contract buyers were victims of an unanticipated shift in macroeconomic policy. It is easy to see how timber contract buyers could have been fooled—macroeconomic conditions were very different in the early 1980s from those in the late 1970s. In an attempt to restore credibility as an inflation fighter, in October 1979 the Federal Reserve announced a shift to new operating procedures and pursued a contractionary monetary policy. The ensuing contraction was sharp, increasing the potential disruption to individuals who failed to respond to the monetary policy shift. The decline in demand for coastal lumber that undermined timber values was not idiosyncratic to that regional industry; nationwide, there was a decrease in housing construction.

Macroeconomic Policy Was Blamed

As the timber contract crisis worsened, the wrath of the Pacific Northwest turned toward economic policymakers in Washington, D.C. For example, in August 1982, Victor Atiyeh, the governor of Oregon at that time, vented his anger in an eloquent speech before a congressional committee that was considering timber contract legislation. Atiyeh argued,

> Oregon did not lead the charge for exorbitant interest rates. Oregon did not dismantle the Nation's traditional sources of mortgage financing.

Oregon had no part in the faustian bargains that plunged this nation into recession. Why, then, is it that Oregon must be bled white on the sacrificial altar of trial and error solutions?[1]

Atiyeh pleaded for relief, for a change in the circumstances that were keeping Oregonians unemployed. Implicitly, he also was arguing that the whole fiasco never would have happened if a radical change in macroeconomic policy had not taken place.

Other advocates of timber contract modification argued that timber contract prices would not have escalated to nonviable levels if the impending course of macroeconomic policy had been known. For example, in a law review article on contract modification, Hampton and Wood (1983) cited the switch in Federal Reserve operating procedures and more zealous advocacy of monetary growth restraint as a particularly damaging policy shift. The argument that a regime shift was proper grounds for contract modification also was clearly stated in the following exchange between John Hall, vice president of the National Forest Products Association (NFPA), and Senator Howard Metzenbaum during congressional hearings on contract modification:

MR. HALL: The industry by and large does maintain that contracts entered into ought to be performed. Industry also recognizes that there are circumstances when there are changed conditions, in this case in part due to the Government's action, which demand that the contracts be looked at, and that the modification be entered into. ...

SENATOR METZENBAUM: I have some difficulty with the giants of the American economic system who believe in the sanctity of contracts. ... I have a little trouble in understanding how the bastions of conservatism, the defenders of the free enterprise system, the stalwarts of the Republican Party, are in a position to come to Congress and say, hey, look, we have been saying Government ought to keep their nose out of business, but this is different. Now it is we who are being hurt. Let us off the hook, would you please?

MR. HALL: I express my appreciation for your fine comments about our organization and the members. Let me add that when one of the parties to the contract has the ability and exercises the ability to change the conditions under which the contract will be performed, that it is appropriate to modify that contract.

SENATOR METZENBAUM: Now what did the Government do to change those conditions?

MR. HALL: We would assert that in October 1979, the Government, through deliberate action, modified the money [sic] policies of the United States in order to combat inflation, an objective which we felt laudable, but the results of which resulted in a significant increase in the mortgage rates and a dried-up housing economy.[2]

This argument for modification of timber contracts makes sense only if timber buyers would have behaved differently if they had known the impending course of macroeconomic policy.

Macroeconomic Conditions Did Change

The macroeconomic conditions of the early 1980s were very different from those of the late 1970s. In October 1979, the Federal Reserve's Open Market Committee (FOMC) announced that it was adopting new operating procedures that would place more emphasis on controlling growth in monetary aggregates and less emphasis on preventing short-term fluctuations in the Federal Funds rate. The new operating procedures made it possible for the Federal Reserve to adopt a sharply disinflationary monetary contraction, even if this sent short-term interest rates above levels previously regarded as unacceptable.

Low target growth rates for the monetary aggregates also were announced at that time, and in the ensuing three years the growth rate of the real money stock was relatively low. Over the 1970s, the ratio of the narrow monetary aggregate, M1, to the gross national product (GNP) deflator was relatively flat. However, real money balances fell about 1 percent per annum in 1980–82.

Short-term interest rates did take off. During the 1970s, the interest rate on three-month Treasury bills had tended to be very similar to the rate of inflation; the difference between the current quarter Treasury bill rate and the rate of increase in the GNP deflator over the preceding three years was negligible, on average. In contrast, this measure of real short-term interest rates exceeded 5 percentage points, on average, in the period 1980–82.

A deficit-prone fiscal policy was responsible for some of the stimulus to real interest rates. Cuts in effective tax rates were adopted, but federal government spending was not restrained enough to offset the corresponding revenue loss. Average quarterly real GNP growth was slightly negative in 1980–82, and transfer payments increased as the unemployment rate rose. Correspondingly, the real federal deficit quadrupled between the first quarter of 1980 and the last quarter of 1982.

The tight-money, loose-fiscal-policy mix had a disinflationary effect. The GNP deflator slowed to about a $3\frac{1}{2}$ percent annual rate of increase in the last quarter of 1982, after beginning the decade at an $8\frac{3}{4}$ percent pace.

Credibility Was a Problem

The credibility of a new policy is an important determinant of the speed with which people adapt to it. In the early 1980s, the credibility of the Federal Reserve's announced disinflationary monetary policy was undermined in several ways. Most important, some observers found it difficult to believe that the traditional goals of monetary policy—real GNP growth and maintaining a low unemployment rate—would be supplanted by inflation as the dominant macroeconomic policy concern. Second, actual monetary growth rates were so variable that observers had an opportunity to interpret the occasional large increases in monetary growth as a sign of wavering Federal Reserve intentions.

A major economic forecaster for large firms in the forest products industry, the FORSIM service of Data Resources, Inc. (DRI), expressed doubts about the Federal Reserve's credibility on the grounds that the Federal Reserve would not abandon its traditional objectives. FORSIM wrote,

> In what some of the more volatile reporters of the economic scene have called an outburst of monetarist brinkmanship the unthinkable has happened: the Federal Reserve has tightened credit in the midst of a recession in which unemployment is close to double-digit territory and many efficient plants and other productive resources lie unused.[3]

FORSIM reported that the key condition underlying its previous housing start forecasts was the eminently rational assumption, in Otto Eckstein's words, "that the Federal Reserve really will become seriously preoccupied with the recession, and will, in a pragmatic way, reconcile the obvious short-run needs of the economy with the pursuit of the Fed's long-range anti-inflationary goals."[4] Apparently, lack of credibility did lengthen the transition period for these professional forecasters.

Monetary growth was highly variable during the early phases of the contraction. Technical problems with monetary control, not wavering intentions, appear to have been responsible for the variability.[5] Nevertheless, this variability may have further undermined the Federal Reserve's credibility (Blanchard, 1984).

Contraction Was Sharp

The fact that there was a credibility problem raises the possibility that much less disruption of real economic activity would have occurred if the announced policy had been believed. According to this interpretation, the severity of the monetary contraction was not in and of itself a major cause of misallocation of resources. Agents were making plans that were optimal in the context of the former policies, and they would have made plans that were optimal in the context of the new policies if they had truly believed that the change was imminent. Thus, there was a need for gradualism in the move toward monetary restraint only because such a move lacked full credibility.

A contrasting interpretation of the disinflationary experience was presented in the 1986 *Economic Report of the President*. In the report of the Council of Economic Advisers (CEA), which traditionally accompanies the president's statement, the CEA argued that the Federal Reserve's decision to bring on such a severe contraction of money and credit was a major policy error. The CEA did agree that the economic costs of disinflation were larger than necessary because the deceleration of monetary growth was too variable to convince the public that the Federal Reserve was committed to a disinflationary policy. This first error purportedly was compounded by the sharpness of the contraction. The CEA noted that despite the Reagan Administration's recommendation that the deceleration in money growth be gradual as well as predictable, there were two six-month periods during 1981 and early 1982 when nominal M1 growth was negligible. The CEA admonished the Federal Reserve as follows: "To minimize the disruption to real economic activity and hasten the adjustment of inflation expectations, both the gradual and predictable elements of that prescription were believed to be important."[6]

Demand Shift Was Not Idiosyncratic

As explained previously, there were large macroeconomic fluctuations in the early 1980s, and these were often cited as the primary reason for the development of overbids on timber contracts. From a macroeconomic policy perspective, the important issue is whether the divergence between timber contract prices and timber values could have been avoided by the establishment of a more predictable macroeconomic environment. The argument that the divergence between timber prices and timber values was caused by macroeconomic policy could be ruled out if an idiosyncratic explanation for the large drop in demand for coastal lumber from 1978 to 1982 could be found. The shift in demand for coastal lumber was largely a macroeconomic phenomenon, suggesting a need for directly testing whether timber bid prices were responsive to macroeconomic developments.

A LINKAGE MODEL

A model was developed to determine both whether the shift in lumber demand was a macroeconomic phenomenon and whether timber bid prices were responsive to macroeconomic developments. The model uses an industrial-linkage approach to forecasting the excess of lumber price over timber conversion cost. The equations include identities that explicitly relate the flow of new orders for coastal lumber to the pace of lumber-intensive activities such as housing construction. None of the equations is given a strict behavioral interpretation, however, and atheoretical time-series representations of economic variables are used when they are thought to improve the model's forecasting performance.

The industrial-linkage approach is a way to link models of particular industries to models of the U.S. macroeconomy.[7] In a standard application, the macroeconomic model is used to predict disaggregated final demand, and linkage equations are used to translate the predicted level and composition of final demand into an estimate of industry shipments.[8] Input–output table coefficients can be used to derive the weights that translate final demands into industry shipments.

The model presented here follows, in part, the FORSIM model of Cardellichio and Veltkamp (1981). The complete model consists of three blocks of equations. The first block predicts macroeconomic conditions. The second block predicts the pace of housing construction and other lumber-intensive final demands, given the macroeconomic conditions.[9] The third block predicts orders for coastal lumber and the spread between lumber prices and timber conversion costs, given the final demands.

The block of equations used to predict macroeconomic conditions is an unrestricted, fourth-order vector autoregression (VAR). The six variables in this set of equations are inflation rate ($\bar{\Pi}$), real interest rate rate ($R - \bar{\Pi}$), growth rate of constant-dollar GNP (GNP), constant-dollar federal deficit (G), and growth rate of constant-dollar money balances (M).

The model uses the projected path of macroeconomic conditions to predict the pace of housing construction and of other end-use demands for lumber (EUD). These lumber-intensive activities are predicted at a regionally disaggregated level in order to develop a more accurate proxy for the demand for lumber from producers in the Coastal Pacific Northwest. This disaggregation was deemed to be useful because, for example, strong housing construction activity in the West provides more of a stimulus to demand for coastal lumber than strong housing construction activity in the Northeast—coastal producers capture a larger share of the western market. Coastal producers' share of lumber demand differs greatly across regional markets because the cost of shipping lumber transcontinentally is high relative to the availability of substitutes.

The consumption region boundaries in the United States follow Census Bureau definitions of the Northeast, North Central, South, and West. The rest of the world is treated as a fifth and final consumption region.

Five explicit indicators of end-use activity are used: single-unit housing starts (EUD_1), multiunit housing starts (EUD_2), mobile-home shipments (EUD_3), nonresidential construction expenditures (EUD_4), and expenditures on residential repairs and alterations (EUD_5). Softwood lumber exports from Oregon and Washington custom districts is used as the sole end-use activity indicator for the rest-of-the-world consumption region (EUD_6).

End-use activity indicators are translated into lumber volume denominations according to a time series of softwood lumber "use factors," as in the FORSIM model. The variation in the use factors across regions is substantial. For example, in 1978 each million units of multiunit starts in the West is assumed to create a demand for twice as much softwood lumber as a million units of multiunit starts in the Northeast.[10] The variation in the use factors across types of end-use demand also are substantial. For example, in 1978 each million units of single-unit starts in the West is assumed to create a demand for almost twice as much softwood lumber as a million units of multiunit starts in the same region.

The levels of lumber demand in the consumption regions are allocated to coastal producers according to a time series of estimates of market share.[11] Coastal lumber producers deliver primarily to markets in the West, but their share of the North Central market also is significant. In 1978, coastal producers captured about 36 percent of softwood lumber sales in the West and 18 percent of lumber sales in the North Central region. Coastal producers captured only about 13 percent of softwood orders in the South and 8 percent of orders in the Northeast.

The model separates each of the national end-use variables into a trend component and a cyclical component. The trends were modeled as a deterministic function of time, as an unobserved random trend, or as a more complicated function, depending on observable variables such as demographic conditions. Deviations from the fitted trends were modeled as functions of macroeconomic conditions and the recent history of the end-use variable in question.

The path of interest rates and real GNP growth were used to predict deviations of housing starts and mobile-home shipments from their trends. This portion of the model required an auxiliary equation to translate the projected path for the short-term Treasury bill interest rate into a projected path for mortgage interest rates. Real GNP growth was the sole macroeconomic variable used to predict the deviations from trend of the other end-use variables.

The model uses the projected path of the end-use variables to predict orders for coastal lumber and timber conversion values. The timber conversion value (X) is defined of the excess of coastal lumber price over capital rental costs and average variable manufacturing and logging costs. Timber conversion value is the maximum amount that a coastal lumber producer could pay for timber and still get a normal economic profit.[12] Since lumber orders are more highly correlated with timber values deflated by manufacturing and logging costs (Z) than with current dollar timber values (X), separate equations for current dollar and deflated timber values are used.

The most important property of the model is its representation of how the expected conversion value evolves with economic conditions. This dependence can be described by calculating the extent to which the model's forecast of future timber values changes when there is unanticipated strength or weakness in a particular economic indicator. The extent of unanticipated strength or weakness is indicated by the magnitude of the error term in the equation for the particular economic indicator.

Table 2-1 summarizes the impact of various error realizations on the model's prediction of twelve-quarter-ahead conversion values. For example, the entry for EUD_1 indicates that the realization of an unexpected 16,808-unit increase in single-unit housing starts in a given quarter would cause the estimate of future timber values to be

TABLE 2-1

Impact Multipliers for Timber Value Projections[a]

Equation[b]	Response[c]	Shock Size[d]
$\Delta \log (MLC)$	3.445	0.002
Z	0.565	0.095
QRESID	0.358	104.952
EUD_1	0.351	16.808
EUD_2	1.993	14.849
EUD_3	0.838	7.573
EUD_4	1.816	3.844
EUD_5	0.906	8.821
EUD_6	0.236	21.689
RM	-0.200	0.001
G	0.034	0.128
GNP	-0.982	0.028
Π	0.925	0.018
M	-0.752	0.042
$R-\bar{\Pi}$	-1.022	0.005

[a] Response of $E_t X_{t+12}$ to a shock in the residual for the specified equation. Shocks are not orthogonalized.

[b] See the model and data appendix for variable definitions.

[c] Multipliers were calculated about the 1967:2 (second quarter),–1979:4 (fourth quarter) sample means of 75.7 for MLC and 1.07 for Z. The 1979:4 values of the γ_{it} were used.

[d] Shock size is 1 asymptotic standard error.

Source: Calculations by the author.

raised by 35 cents. These impact multipliers have the anticipated signs. Positive innovations in the deflated timber value or in any of the end-use demands increase the model's estimate of future timber values. A positive innovation in the nominal mortage rate reduces the model's estimate of future timber values.[13]

THE DROP IN COASTAL LUMBER ORDERS

Short-run fluctuations in lumber prices are largely caused by changes in lumber demand. The 1978–82 slide in lumber prices coincided with a reduction in new orders for coastal lumber from a peak of 8.9 BBF in 1978 to a trough of 6.0 BBF in 1982. This one-third decrease in coastal orders over four years was the largest and longest decrease of the 1960s and 1970s.[14] An understanding of the reasons for the drop in lumber orders is essential to figuring out whether optimistic macro-economic policy assumptions were a primary cause of the large overbids on timber contracts. If the drop in coastal lumber orders was caused by an event specific to the coastal region, say a decline in market share, then it would be inappropriate to blame it on macroeconomic conditions.

In fact, coastal producers did lose market share over 1978–82, but most of the drop in lumber orders can be traced to the nationwide decline in housing construction and other end-use activities. The easiest way to trace the drop in lumber orders is to consider a group of counterfactual scenarios.

Scenario 1. Start with the fact that national-level single-unit housing starts fell more than 50 percent between 1978 and 1982. Hold constant at 1978 levels other end-use activities, the regional composition of end-use activity, use factors, and coastal market share. Determine how much of the one-third drop in coastal orders can be explained by the observed 50 percent drop in national single-unit housing starts.

Scenario 2. Start with the fact that national-level multiunit housing starts fell about one-third between 1978 and 1982. Hold constant at 1978 levels other end-use activities, the regional composition of end-use activity, use factors, and coastal market share. Determine how much of the one-third drop in coastal orders can be explained by the observed drop in national multiunit housing starts.

Scenario 3. Let coastal market share vary as it did between 1978 and 1982. Hold constant at 1978 levels end-use activities, the regional

TABLE 2-2

Decomposition of the Drop in Coastal Lumber Orders Between 1978 and 1982

Source	Lost Volume[a] (BBF)	Lost Volume Relative to All Sources (percent)
End-use demands (EUD)	2.3	0.78
Market share of producers	1.0	0.34
Regional shares of EUD	0.5	0.17
Use factors	0.0	0.04
All sources	2.9	100

[a]Change in orders between 1978 and 1982.

Source: Calculations by the author (Mattey, 1988).

composition of end-use activity, and use factors. Determine how much of the one-third drop in coastal orders can be explained by the observed changes in market share.

One can see from these calculations that most of the change in coastal orders can be explained at the national end-use activity level. As a group, the observed variation in national end-use demand between 1978 and 1982 explains about three-fourths of the reduction in coastal orders (Table 2-2). Changes in the relationship of regional end-use activity to national aggregate activity explain less than 20 percent of the reduction in coastal orders. Changes in use factors had little net effect on coastal orders. At the 1978 level of regional softwood lumber demand, changes in market share account for about one-third of the reduction in coastal orders.[15] Thus changes in market share were significant, but the decrease in national end-use activity was the most important cause of the reduction in coastal orders.

Opposing Evidence

Timber Prices Exceeded Projected Values

In view of the close link between macroeconomic activity and end-use demands such as housing construction, the preceding analysis suggests that the low lumber prices and timber values of 1982 may have been caused primarily by depressed macroeconomic conditions. The demonstration that industry-specific developments were not the primary source of the reduction in demand for coastal lumber lends plausibility to the claim that timber contracts would not have been overbid if a radical change in macroeconomic policy had not taken place. However, the question of whether timber buyers actually would have bid much less if they knew about the coming macroeconomic policy changes remains unanswered.

To investigate how timber bids might have changed if macroeconomic policy had been more predictable, it is useful to consider how the model's forecasts of future timber conversion values evolve. If the model were greatly fooled by the unpredictable macroeconomic conditions of the early 1980s, and if the bids of timber buyers were consistent with the forecasts of the model, the claim that timber buyers were fooled by the shift in macroeconomic policy would gain credence.

To embody pre-1980 macroeconomic conditions in the forecasting properties of the model, the quarterly data used in estimating the unknown parameters of the model are extended only through the last quarter of 1979. At the given values of the estimated parameters, the model's forecasts of twelve-quarter-ahead timber values are derived from the usual formulas for the conditional expectation of a variable in a dynamic linear model, using data through the current quarter.[16]

Figure 2-1 depicts the model's projection of twelve-quarter-ahead timber conversion values and actual timber contract bid prices. According to the model, timber contract prices should have started to drop in the third quarter of 1979 and fallen well below $100/MBF, LT by the fourth quarter of 1980. Actual bid prices continued to climb through the first quarter of 1980 and stayed above $200/MBF, LT until the third quarter of 1981. These results suggest two conclusions: The model was not greatly fooled by the unpredictable macroeconomic conditions of the early 1980s, and the bids of timber buyers were not consistent with the forecasts of the model.

The conclusion that the bids of timber buyers were too high to be explained by model-based forecasts is fairly robust. The conclusion is robust to alternative specifications of the forecasting model, including the use of univariate and bivariate autoregressions, and to the incorporation of uncertainty about parameter estimates.[17]

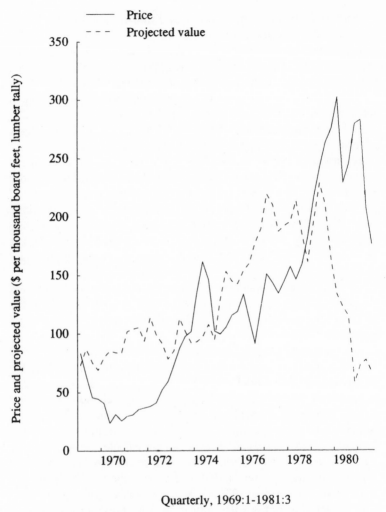

Quarterly, 1969:1-1981:3

FIGURE 2-1. Douglas-fir timber price versus projected value.

Figure 2-2 shows actual timber contract bid prices and an upper bound for twelve-quarter-ahead projections of timber values. The upper bound incorporates parameter uncertainty as well as residual variance. The upper bound was calculated by Monte Carlo methods[18]; in 95 percent of the draws from the distribution of

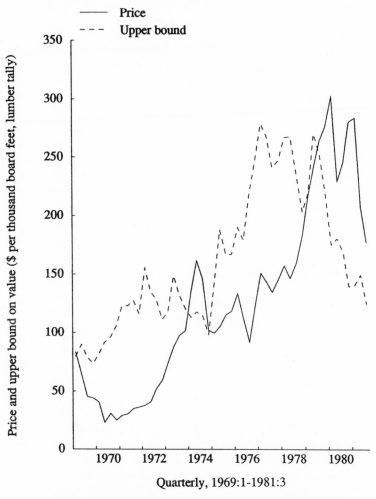

FIGURE 2-2. Price versus upper bound on projected value.

unknown parameters, the model projections were less than the plotted upper bound. As shown in Figure 2-2, actual bid prices moved above the upper bound in the third quarter of 1979 and remained so through the third quarter of 1981. During this period, the bids of timber buyers were too high to be explained by the model-based projections of timber values.

Barriers to Fast Adaptation Existed

Apparently, timber contract buyers did not adapt quickly to changing macroeconomic conditions. The slow pace of adaptation probably can be traced to specific barriers to fast adaptation. For example, arbitrage in the market for federal timber is limited by timber sale procedures and the expense of transporting sawn logs. Prior to the early 1980s, timber buyers could have been unsophisticated about macroeconomic policy without being driven to the edge of insolvency. The crucial expectations of timber buyers are expectations about the prices they will be able to receive for products made from timber. Fast adaptation to a new macroeconomic environment would have required an understanding of the complicated linkage between macroeconomic policy and product prices.

The kind of barriers to fast adaptation that existed in the federal timber market have been recognized by others as impeding adaptation to regime shifts. For example, Mankiw, Miron, and Weil (1987) discussed similar considerations in a study of the pace of adaptation to the founding of the Federal Reserve. These authors argued that the creation of the Federal Reserve caused a major change in the behavior of short-term (three-month) interest rates and that longer-term (six-month) interest rates quickly embodied the new short-rate process, as measured by a term–structure relation. In presenting a number of caveats to a general interpretation of their results, they first noted that the results are not necessarily indicative of the expectations of all participants in asset markets. Since arbitrage by a well-informed subset of the participants in the New York short-term loan market could have produced the results, "One should be cautious in applying our findings to situations in which the relevant expectations are those of a larger or less sophisticated group of economic actors".[19] Secondly, the implications of the regime change for the short-term credit markets were relatively easy to predict. Interest rate stability was one of the announced goals of Fed policy, and the results of Mankiw et al. show that the market correctly anticipated greater stability. But "in many other cases of regime changes, the crucial expectations are those of nontarget variables. In these cases, the relevant economic actors must have an implicit or explicit model of the economy, which complicates their problem of understanding the new regime".[20]

The timber contract overbidding episode suggests that gradualism is important in macroeconomic policy because barriers to fast adaptation exist in some markets. The overbidding on coastal USFS timber contracts in the years 1979 through 1981 cannot be fully explained by the shift in macroeconomic policy. Timber prices rose too quickly and stayed high for too long. A more gradual monetary contraction and less deficit-prone fiscal policy probably would have prevented some of the divergence between timber contract prices and ex post facto timber contract values, by holding the timber contract values up.

3

Risk-Taking by Zombie Firms?

The "zombie effect" is the additional incentive to borrow funds and make risky investments created by insolvency of a firm. The zombie effect can be neutralized by risk sensitivity in the cost of credit to the insolvent firm. It can be quite strong if the insolvent firm can obtain credit at risk-insensitive costs and receives temporary forebearance from a closure rule that depends on the firm's net worth position. This chapter explores whether the timber contract overbidding can be explained as rational risk-taking by zombie firms.

Zombie Effect in a Bankruptcy Model

The basic features of the zombie effect can be illustrated in the context of a variant of the Bulow and Shoven (1978) model of bankruptcy.[1] The model helps illustrate why an insolvent firm that has received temporary forebearance from closure has an incentive to undertake risky investments. Such a firm would not be interested in raising the capital to make such investments if the rate it pays on new liabilities fully reflects any increased risk of default.

The model represents a firm that currently has low net worth and insufficient cash to meet all current liabilities. Bankruptcy will occur immediately if the firm cannot raise additional cash. There are three classes of risk-neutral claimants to the firm: bondholders, a bank lender, and equity holders. The distinguishing feature of the bondholder class is that its claims cannot be renegotiated. The bank has the option of either granting additional loans to the troubled firm or forcing it into bankruptcy. The equity holders have the residual claims on the value of the firm, and this value currently is near zero.

Thus the equity holders will be willing to offer the bank some of the gains they might make if the firm survives in exchange for an emergency infusion of cash.

At the beginning of the first period, the firm has cash (liquid assets) in amount C_0 and tangible assets such as plant and equipment that could be liquidated for sum V_0^L. The firm's liabilities include a payment of $r_d D$ dollars in interest on bonds, due now; a payment of $r_b B$ dollars in interest on the bank loan, due now; and repayment of the $B + D$ dollars of principal due on these borrowings, payable at the end of the first period. If the firm operates in a period t, it generates net operating earnings in amount Z_t that are received at the end of the period. For analytical convenience we can collapse the discounted stream of expected net operating earnings into a single variable

$$V_t^z = E_t \sum_{i=0}^{\infty} \beta^i Z_{t+i}$$

The discounted stream of expected net operating earnings, V_t^z, is the only source of uncertainty in the model. For expositional simplicity, let us take the discount rate, β, to be unity. It is assumed that if the firm survives the current-period financial crisis, at the end of the first period the equity interest in the firm will be sold to a fourth party for the excess of the expected operating value of the firm, V_1^z, over any outstanding net indebtedness.

The firm negotiates with the bank for a loan in the amount of $B^* = C_0 - r_d D - r_b B$ to meet current obligations. The loan principal and interest of $(1 + r^*)B^*$ for the new loan would be due at the end of period one.

The firm is willing to accept the loan as long as the interest rate on the loan, r^*, does not exceed the threshold at which the meager or nonexistent proceeds from liquidating the firm now, max $\{0, [V_0^L + C_0 - (1 + r_d)D - (1 + r_b)B]\}$, exceed the expected discounted value of the equity payoff under continued operations. The latter expected value incorporates two possibilities:

1. If the operating value of the firm, V_1^z, turns out to be less than the net indebtedness, $(1 + r_d)D + (1 + r_b)B(1 + r^*)B^* - C_0$, the bank and bondholders will split the operating value of the firm in proportion to their share of the total liabilities of the firm and the equity owners will get zero.

2. If the operating value of the firm turns out to exceed the net
   indebtedness, the bank and bondholders will be paid off in full and
   the equity owners will keep the residual.

The bank is willing to grant the loan as long as the interest rate, r^*,
does not fall short of the threshold at which its expected return from
the firm being allowed to continue operations is at least as great as its
expected return under current liquidation.

Golbe (1988) explored the bankruptcy model in the case when
the firm's current net worth is negative, $[V_0^L + C_0 - (1 + r_d)D - (1 + r_b)B)] < 0$. Golbe showed that if the bank grants the firm a loan
to continue operations, a mean preserving spread in the distribution of
V_1^z cannot decrease the expected payoff for the coalition of bank and
equity owners. This coalition may gain from increased risk because it
captures all abnormally high returns and has a limit on the amount
that can be lost. The bondholders cannot gain from increased risk
because they will not share in any returns beyond those that allow full
payment of the fixed bond debt. Golbe (1988) did not model how the
coalition of bank and equity holders might split expected gains to
continued operations, a split that is governed by the value of the
interest rate on the new loan, r^*.

The zombie effect arises in situations where r^* does not incorporate
increases in the risk that the loan will be defaulted. In the context of
the bankruptcy model just described, this risk insensitivity can be
represented as the bank's offering the loan at an interest rate r^* that is
expected to produce profits at the existing distribution of expected
operating profits V_1^z but not preventing the firm from assuming more
risk. Once the interest rate on the new loan is fixed, the bank is in the
same position as the bondholders; the equity owners have an
incentive to induce a mean-preserving spread in the distribution of
V_1^z. In this sense, the nearly insolvent firm has the incentive to attract
loans at risk-insensitive rates and to invest the acquired funds in risky
assets.

Zombie Effect in the Thrift Industry

In some ways, the role of the Forest Service in the timber contract
bailout is similar to that of the Federal Home Loan Bank Board
(FHLBB) in the recent thrift industry bailout. Both agencies chose to

grant insolvent firms forebearance from policies that would have led to closure; both agencies failed to restrict access to credit that could be obtained at risk-insensitive costs.

Agencies that have the authority to enforce closure of insolvent firms face a dilemma. Often the insolvent firm provides services or employment that specific businesses or households consider essential, and the closure of the firm disrupts these services or employment. However, closing the insolvent firm limits the potential losses of the creditors to current levels. If the firm is allowed to continue to operate, the existing assets might be completely dissipated and additional liabilities incurred. Furthermore, failure to close an insolvent firm can irreparably harm the credibility of the controlling agency, especially if it means explicit forebearance from a previously established policy.

Throughout the 1980s, the FHLBB faced the dilemma of whether to close insolvent thrift institutions. Many such thrifts were allowed to continue to operate, partially because the FHLBB and the Federal Savings and Loan Insurance Corporation (FSLIC) did not have enough resources to dispose of troubled thrifts quickly.[2] Recently, Congress has agreed to massive federal expenditures in an effort to resolve the thrift industry crisis.

Even before the current thrift crisis it was widely recognized that a deposit insurance system with risk-insensitive premiums creates a moral hazard. The financial institution has an extra incentive to adopt a risky portfolio because the introduction of deposit insurance eliminates the need for depositors to demand a risk premium. Instead of basing deposit insurance premiums on the risk to the insurance fund, bank and thrift regulators have attempted to directly limit the riskiness of financial institution portfolios by establishing net worth requirements and other standards. Regulators have the authority to take control of a financial institution that fails to meet the standards; since the net worth requirements exceed zero, the prompt exercise of this authority can prevent losses to the insurance funds.

A number of economists have argued that the total cost of closing down insolvent thrifts has increased significantly because the thrifts were allowed to continue to operate. Insolvent thrifts aggressively sought more deposits and placed the acquired funds in risky investments. They behaved like zombies, striking terror into the hearts of living, solvent thrifts that had to compete with them for deposits.[3]

Zombie Effect in the Timber Market

The bankruptcy model just presented is too simplified to be taken as
an empirical specification of the zombie effect in the timber market.
Furthermore, to test specifically for the significance of the zombie
effect in the timber market, time-series data on firm balance sheet
characteristics and timber contract acquisitions would be needed.
While the necessary time-series data on timber contract acquisitions
are available, only an end-of-episode snapshot of firm balance sheets
is available. Therefore, instead of formally testing for the significance
of the zombie effect, this chapter uses an alternative strategy for
analyzing the empirical evidence. This strategy is to identify characteristics that are likely to be correlated with a firm's incentive to
assume risk on timber contracts, and then to see if the distribution of
overbidding across firms is correlated with the selected characteristics. The bankruptcy model suggests that, other things being equal,
firms with low liquidation values have more incentive to assume risk.

Excess Capacity

The liquidation value of a lumber mill depends greatly on its location.
A mill in an area where mill capacity outstrips the available supply of
timber is not worth nearly as much as a mill in an area where timber is
abundant. Thus, it is important to investigate whether there is a
significant spatial dimension to the overbidding on timber contracts.

Timber prices accelerated more in the Coastal Pacific Northwest
than in other regions of the United States. If the high timber prices of
1979–81 were based on optimistic expectations about macroeconomic conditions, and expectations were homogeneous across
regions, then large overbids in other regions also would have been
observed.[4] Something unique was happening in the coastal region.

The USDA offered the following explanation for why the largest
bid acceleration occurred in the coastal region:

> [M]any mills in this region own little or no forest lands and are heavily
> dependent upon Federal timber as their source of raw material. This
> dependency has increased over the past two decades as privately owned
> mature timber available for purchase has been harvested. The expectation
> of the forest products industry, and particularly of those mill operators
> who owned little or no timber was that, as timber from private sources

became scarce, increasing volumes would be made available from the accumulated large inventories of old growth timber on western Federal forest lands, particularly on the Pacific Coast. In fact, Federal timber sales did gradually increase from 1950 until 1969, but have remained virtually at the same level for the last 13 years. ... Thus, because the Federal Government did not sell timber in volumes sufficient to support existing mill capacity, and there was insufficient volume of private timber in certain areas, excessive bidding by mill owners occurred with each trying to acquire an adequate supply of raw material. The competition for limited timber offerings has been fierce. The operator with timber under contract at least had a hope of protecting his investment, whereas the one without timber was forced to close his operation and to liquidate his mill facility.[5]

The USDA makes two important assertions here. The first claim is that in particular subregions of the Coastal Pacific Northwest, industry-level capacity became excessive relative to timber supply. The second claim is that, given timber prices that would have cleared the market in the absence of this excess capacity, individual firms in these subregions preferred to assume the risk of encountering losses on federal timber contracts over closing their operations and selling the plant and equipment. The other assertions are offered as partial explanations for how this excess capacity could have developed and for why the federal timber market would clear at a higher price in the presence of excess capacity. The zombie effect is a potential explanation for why a higher price for timber was necessary to clear the market, given the excess capacity.

The USDA argued that many firms had made large investments in plant and equipment under the assumption that public timber sales volumes would increase as private inventories of mature timber dwindled. When public timber sales volumes failed to increase and legislative developments threatened to permanently stifle public timber sales growth by expanding the portion of national forests reserved as wilderness areas, expectations about future sales volumes were revised downward. Such a shift in expectations created a need for industry-level disinvestment, because industry-level production plans had to be revised downward in response to the reduced timber supply.

While disinvestment of plant and equipment was necessary for the coastal forest products industry as a whole, disinvestment by each firm was not desirable. Disinvestment by each firm would have placed some firms in a region of the production technology where there are increasing returns to scale; the industry as a whole could have obtained larger expected profits by completely shutting down some mills and leaving others operating at higher, more efficient output levels. Presumably, the USDA's statement that each firm attempted to obtain an "adequate" supply of timber means that no firm was willing to obtain a supply of timber that would leave it producing at grossly inefficient output levels.

Many individual firms perceived that they had only two alternatives: to liquidate their entire capital stock or to maintain a timber inventory that would support operating at efficient levels. These firms did not necessarily adjust their inventory targets in response to changes in the cost of acquiring timber or to revisions in expectations about product prices. Because the technology of the mills was fixed in the short run, firms that adhered to the strategy of maintaining enough timber to support efficient output levels were relatively insensitive to changes in timber bid prices and in expected product prices. For example, John Davis of Williamette Industries admitted,

> We did not become involved in this intense bidding just because we felt the inflationary spiral of the times would go on and on indefinitely. Rather, it was a case of buy the timber now so that we would have the logs to operate with 3 to 5 years in the future.[6]

How are plant closures determined in an atomistic manufacturing industry with excess capacity? In the coastal forest products industry, the market for federal timber functioned as a lottery for determining which firms would exit. James Geisinger, a representative of one firm, recounted how "they faced the fact that several companies had to face at the same time, that there are basically two ways to go out of business in our industry. One is to have no timber to process, and the other is to have timber that may be too costly to process."[7] For firms without access to private timber, forced exit from the industry was certain if no public timber contracts were purchased. A company that purchased timber contracts at least had a chance of getting lucky. The incentive to gamble on the timber contracts depended on the liquidation value of the firm—on how much would be lost if timber conversion values failed to appreciate.

Specific Human Capital and Implicit Contracts

In testimony before Congress, the existence of specific human capital was widely cited as a disincentive to liquidation. Some mill owners would have been forced to abandon their occupation if they sold their mill. Owner/managers who had made investments in their own human capital, "learning the business," sought to preserve the return on this investment. For example, James Stock of Clear Lumber Company told Congress, "I represent another one of those family-owned lumber companies. I'm second generation, with the third coming on. My family assets are totally committed to the industry, it's what we know how to do."[8]

Mill owners appear to have had a broad conception of the nature of their forest products firms; often this conception included a commitment to employment stability. Mills tend to be spatially close to mature commercial timber lands because logs are costly to transport. Some mills were constructed near remote national forests to achieve this proximity, and the housing stock and public-service facilities in adjacent communities grew to meet the demands of the mills' labor force. The investment in the development of a viable mill town was much greater than the investment in the mill itself.

Mill workers in mill towns generally valued stability of employment at their current job more than typical urban workers. The lack of alternative employment opportunities in the mill towns created a demand for stability both because dismissed workers had individual difficulty in obtaining alternative labor income and because the concurrent reduction in the town's aggregate labor income created capital losses on real property such as the housing stock. Daniel Goldy testified that as director of economic development for Oregon he learned that

> given the persistent shortage of timber, mills that go bankrupt or close down because of timber problems rarely if ever change ownerships and operate again. ... If the companies are forced into default and bankruptcy, the real victims will be the workers and the communities who have been dependent on those companies for their livelihood. For many communities who will lose their only operating payroll, it means a devastating loss of value in homes, Main Street property, investments in infrastructure, and ultimately economic disaster for the entire community.[9]

Mill owners and workers in small mill towns had an implicit contract to keep employment stable in order to avoid economic disaster in their communities

James Stock testified that his family-owned firm was living up to such a commitment to employment stability:

> My family, and others like us, have continued to express our commit-
> ment to our communities. ... All through this economic recession we have
> kept our plants operating and our people working, despite the fact we are
> losing money. ... The only possible light at the end of the tunnel in these
> times is a less expensive timber base. We are committed to operate and
> deplete our assets as long as it is possible.[10]

Stock's commitment to the community apparently made him reluct-ant to shut down the mill and encouraged him to gamble on the timber contracts.

The SBA Ratchet Effect

A firm's incentive to assume timber debt instead of liquidating also was affected by its size as measured by the number of persons it employed. The Small Business Administration (SBA) sponsors a timber sale set-aside program that is implemented by the USFS. The program's purpose is to preserve small business firms by reducing their costs of acquiring timber and by establishing a disincentive to mergers and acquisitions that would increase firm size.[11]

The program sets aside tracts of timber to be sold exclusively to SBA-eligible firms. To be eligible for set-aside sales, a firm must be primarily engaged in the logging or forest products industry, be independently owned and operated, and have fewer than 500 employees. Set-aside sales are triggered when SBA-eligible firms fail to acquire a prespecified "base" share of the total sales offered. No more than 30 percent of the logs from a set-aside sale may be resold to non-SBA-eligible manufacturers; the limitation on resale ensures that the program benefits small manufacturers, not just small logging firms.

The geographic unit used in defining a small-business share is called a market area. In most national forests in the coastal region there are two or three market areas. The initial base share was computed as the small firms' average share of timber volume purchased in 1966 to 1970. The base shares were recomputed at five-year intervals, and one of these intervals ended on September 30, 1980. Set-aside sales were triggered in semiannual evaluations.

The difference between small firms' actual purchases and guaranteed purchases is called the SBA volume deficit. If this deficit was 10 percent or more of guaranteed purchases at an evaluation date, set-aside sales were to be offered until the accumulating deficit was less than the 10 percent threshold. At the half-decade dates when base shares were recomputed, the volume deficit was to be carried forward if the recomputation of the base share would alter the base share by less than 5 percentage points.[12] Otherwise, the USFS and local SBA representative were to make an administrative decision about the disposition of the volume deficit. Usually the entire deficit was dropped.[13]

The existence of the set-aside program affected timber bidding incentives in two ways. First, because a mill that was run by a small firm had privileged access to federal timber, ceteris paribus a mill was more valuable to a small firm than to a large firm. Second, the method of recomputing the base shares created a "ratchet effect" that provided small firms with an incentive to expand the volume of timber purchased at the end of the five-year period. Any increase in small firms' actual share for the 1976–80 period would increase their guaranteed volume over 1981–85. However, unless the increase was greater than 5 percentage points, the increase in the guaranteed volume from the base share change would be partially offset by carryover of the volume deficit. Large firms had an interest in preventing increases in the SBA base share in their market area. The manipulation of volumes tended to occur at the end of the five-year periods because the opposing groups had the least opportunity to respond them.

The SBA ratchet effect was explicitly cited as a cause of timber price escalation by some timber buyers. Edward Hines reported that the base share recomputation method added to the upward pressure on bids because large non-timber-owning companies "were compelled to bid high prices just to assure sufficient supply to keep their mills operating."[14] Forrest Dobson recounted that large firms were not always successful in protecting their share:

In some instances, and we are well aware of one in particular, this excessive bidding was used to not only accumulate a large backlog of timber under contract, but also as a means to gain more lasting effects. We refer here to the small business set-aside timber sale program. Unrealistically high bids on timber sales in the Chelan marketing area by SBA-sized concerns in the period of 1977–1980 resulted in an inordinate increase in the SBA share of timber sales upon the recalculation in 1980 for the next 5-year period.[15]

This testimony and the nature of the incentives created by the SBA set-aside program suggest that some of the overbidding was caused by the ratchet effect.

Credit Costs Were Insensitive to Risk

Timber buyers would have been less reluctant to liquidate their mills if the cost of buying a timber contract had been explicitly related to the individual risk of default. However, timber buyers could become very highly leveraged in timber contracts, which greatly increased the risk of default, without bearing additional costs to insure the USFS against default. The problem was exacerbated by laws that limit owners' personal liability for corporate debt and that allow declaration of bankruptcy: An insolvent timber buyer could increase his or her stake in timber contracts, knowing full well that any contingent liabilities created by the additional timber contracts would never be paid.

Deposits on timber contracts were minimal. To participate in the bidding one needed to furnish the sale administrator a token amount by cashier's check or "bid bond." One purpose of this deposit was to prevent a bidder from running up the price in the oral auction and then refusing to accept the award of the contract at that price in writing. The bid bond deposit was refunded to those who were not the high bidder on the sale.

To be awarded the sale and not lose the bid bond, the high bidder was required to submit a deposit in cash or "performance bond" in an amount that covered the costs of completing work required of the purchaser after a logging season was completed, such as soil erosion prevention and road maintenance. Usually this was 5 percent of the total bid.

On the typical contracts in the coastal region, payment was made as the timber was cut. The purchaser maintained an account with the

USFS with a target balance that roughly equaled the price of the amount of timber that could be cut in thirty to sixty days. As timber was harvested and scaled, the account was debited and the purchaser was billed enough to restore the target balance.

The purchaser's liability for default charges was insufficiently secured under this system of payments and deposits. Implicitly, the liability for the default charges was secured by the buyer's personal or corporate assets. There were no explicit collateral requirements other than the minimal performance bond. Thus the cost of acquiring the timber contracts was not sensitive to default risk.

The insensitivity of the deposit requirements to the risk of purchaser default created an incentive for some firms to gamble on the timber contracts instead of liquidating their mills. The expected return on a basket of timber contracts was larger for highly leveraged firms. Bankruptcy could be used to truncate losses, and the acquisition cost was insensitive to the degree of leverage.

Apparently, the ease of getting in on a big gamble attracted some pure speculators. For example, Fred Sohn noted, "During the heydays of the bidding we even had a used car dealer, with absolutely no interest in the industry, successfully bid a major timber sale running out all competitors."[16] Anna Bevens explained,

> The speculators came into the market without adequate facilities to cut the timber they contracted for but with the intention of holding it. As the price accelerated it permitted them to sell logs or third party the sale with considerable profits, to a mill who had been unable to buy at the bidding table.[17]

C. Donald Fisher, a representative of one of the larger firms in the industry, bemoaned that these timber sale practices left legitimate producers quite vulnerable:

> With our $100 million investment in plants we endeavored to maintain a 2 to 3-year supply of timber ahead for rational planning purposes. To do this, we and others were forced to compete against fast buck speculators with no plant facilities who were looking for what appeared to them to be a pot of gold at the end of the rainbow.[18]

The inadequacy of the payment and deposit system is most glaringly apparent when an individual with little capital at risk threatens to outbid a firm that has $100 million in assets that could serve as collateral.

However, because the timber contract liabilities were not collatera- lized, a legitimate producer who faced insolvency, perhaps from losses on earlier timber contracts, had the same incentive as the pure speculator to increase the stake of the gamble on timber contracts. Large firms with diversified operations were less likely to become insolvent from losses on timber contracts because income and assets from outside operations were affected less by a downturn in the lumber market.

Patterns in Timber Contract Overbids

Records of individual timber sales and data on the characteristics of individual firms and the coastal forest products industry were used to quantify the importance of excess capacity in explaining the timber contract overbids and to identify which of the disincentives to liquidation were most significant. The timber price escalation func- tioned as a probabilistic mechanism for determining which firms would exit. Since the number of exiting firms increases with the extent of overbidding, overbids on timber contracts needed to be largest in those subregions of the Coastal Region with the most excess capacity.

To construct meaningful measures of excess capacity, the Coastal Region was disaggregated into six subregions that have been largely self-sufficient in terms of log flows. Three of these subregions are in the state of Washington: Puget Sound, Olympic Peninsula, and Lower Columbia. The other three subregions are in the state of Oregon: Northwest, West Central, and Southwest.[19]

Between 1976 and 1982, the installed single-shift lumber mill capacity of each subregion except the Olympic Peninsula fell more than 10 percent.[20] West central Oregon had the largest rate of disinvestment, over 25 percent. Presumably, more mills had to be shut down in those subregions where expectations about the path of timber supply changed the most. Since such expectations cannot be observed, a proxy for planned disinvestment is needed. This proxy is the fraction of lumber mills that are more than one-third dependent on USFS logs. This proxy by subregion, EXCESSK, has been formed by projecting observed disinvestment rates on dependence on USFS logs.[21]

Table 3-1 presents sample regression coefficients between timber contract overbids, excess capacity, and various characteristics of timber sales and the purchasing firms. The overbid on a contract is calculated as the excess of the bid price over the expected value of the timber at the termination date of the contract.[22]

In the first row of Table 3-1, the simple regression coefficient between timber overbids and a percentage point of planned disinvestment is roughly $20/MBF,LS. This point estimate is almost twenty times its standard error.

However, because the quality of the timber and the costs of harvesting and transporting the timber to the nearest mill can differ greatly across sales, the simple regression coefficient could reflect a systematic differential in sale characteristics across subregions. The USFS makes elaborate appraisals of timber sales, which identify many of the quality and cost differences between the sales. Here, an index of sale quality (QUALITY) is constructed as the ratio of the appraised net rate on the sale to the average appraised net rate on all sales with the same appraisal base period.[23] The second row of Table 3-1 shows that the regression coefficient between OVERBID

TABLE 3-1

Regression Coefficients in Equations for Timber Overbids[a]

Eq.	Excess	Quality	Not Salvage	Not Lgown	Insolvent	Solvent	Ratchet
1	19.9						
	(1.1)						
2	14.1	110.3					
	(1.0)	(5.3)					
3	11.6	109.1	101.7	15.6			
	(1.0)	(5.1)	(7.2)	(7.6)			
4	11.4	108.7	104.4	12.6	34.3	− 39.6	
	(1.0)	(5.1)	(7.2)	(7.7)	(10.4)	(19.8)	
5	11.4	108.7	104.5	14.8	33.7	− 39.1	63.3
	(1.0)	(5.1)	(7.2)	(7.8)	(10.4)	(19.8)	(34.7)

[a] The dependent variable is OVERBID, in $/MBF, LS. The sample consists of 2370 observations on USFS Region 6, Zone 2 contracts bid in 1978:04–1981:03. Equations were estimated by least squares with volume weights (WLS). WLS standard errors are in parentheses. Quarterly time effects and a constant were included in all equations but are not listed in the table. See the text and Mattey (1988) for explanations of column heads and details of data construction.

Source: Calculations by the author.

and EXCESSK falls by about \$6/MBF,LS when QUALITY is included in the regression; apparently, sales have higher quality in those subregions with the most excess capacity.

"Salvage sales" are sales of timber that has to be harvested quickly to prevent destruction of the wood by insects, disease, or other agents. Since the purchaser cannot profitably wait until the end of the contract term to harvest such timber, salvage sales tend to command lower prices. NOT SALVAGE is a dummy variable for nonsalvage sales.[24]

Firms with substantial self-owned timber lands would not have participated in the overbidding on federal timber to avoid reducing production to inefficient capacity utilization levels. Any observed overbids by such firms are more likely to have been caused by overly optimistic expectations about timber conversion values. Data on firms' wood self-sufficiency are readily available for only a few large, publicly held corporations. The variable NOT LGOWN is a dummy that equals 1 unless the firm is one of those identified as relatively self-sufficient.

As displayed in the third row of Table 3-1, the coefficient on EXCESSK falls another \$2.50/MBF, LS when the distribution of salvage sales and large timber owners across subregions is incorporated into the regression. As anticipated, nonsalvage sales and sales not bought by large timber owners commanded higher prices.

The size of the coefficient estimate on NOT LGOWN is difficult to interpret. If timber was homogeneous within each subregion and the markets were being cleared by a Walrasian auctioneer, then large timber-owning firms would have to pay the same stumpage prices as other firms to obtain any USFS timber. Under the actual heterogeneity of the commodity and ascending oral auction sales procedures, the law of one price does not hold. On average, large timber-owning firms made lower quality-adjusted winning bids than the other firms, and their share of timber purchased dropped accordingly.

Several other variables were constructed to investigate the significance of the various disincentives to liquidate. INSOLVENT is a proxy for the extent to which a firm expected to be able to truncate losses by declaring bankruptcy. It equals 1 if the firm qualified for the minimum buyout charge on all the contracts it sought to return to the USFS. To meet the general criterion for minimum buyout charges, a purchaser had to submit a certified statement of net book worth that indicated the firm would be insolvent if forced to pay default penalties based on appraised timber values. SOLVENT identifies firms that bought out of some contracts at non minimum rates. The reference firms subsumed in the constant did not submit buyout applications.

As shown in the fourth row of Table 3-1, firms that are known to have become insolvent tended to overbid $34/MBF,LS more than firms of unknown solvency, ceteris paribus. Firms that were known to be solvent tended to bid substantially less. Some of this observed correlation undoubtedly reflects the fact that firms that overbid for omitted reasons are more likely to have become insolvent. Nevertheless, the large positive correlation between insolvency and overbids is informative. A small correlation would rule out the hypothesis that firms overbid because they expected to be able to truncate losses by declaring bankruptcy.[25] The large positive correlation shows that the hypothesis may be valid.

RATCHET is a proxy for the incentives created by the SBA set-aside program. It equals 1 if the sale is open to all classes of bidders and the winning bidder is a firm in the size class with the most incentive to prevent further drift in the small-business share within the marketing area. More specifically, RATCHET equals 1 for open sales when the absolute value of the difference between actual and base shares is between 5 and 10 percentage points; furthermore, when the difference is negative, the winning firm must have been SBA eligible, and vice versa. After the third quarter of 1980, the RATCHET variable equals 0 for all sales because a new five-year period of base share determination had begun.

As shown in the fifth row of Table 3-1, overbids tended to be much higher ($63/MBF, LS) on open sales where the SBA ratchet effect incentives were the strongest. Although the coefficient is estimated less precisely than those on other variables in the regression, the significance of the ratchet effect cannot be rejected easily.

Additional regressions, not reported in Table 3-1, explored human capital and implicit contract effects. HUMANK is a proxy for the incentive of owner/managers to protect their jobs, their means of earning a return on specific human capital. MILLTOWN is a proxy for the incentive of mill operators in small towns to abide by implicit contracts to stabilize employment. Two observable variables were used to construct these proxies: the population of the town in which the mill is located and the number of manufacturing facilities run by the firm. Human capital effects and implicit contract effects are less likely to be significant for firms with multiple manufacturing facilities. The multiplicity of locations and managers creates competing interests; the multiple-facility firm cannot take a risk in the hope of saving one of the operations without jeopardizing other operations. Implicit contract effects are unlikely to be significant in large towns, but human capital effects may still be present. MILLTOWN equals 1 if the firm is a manufacturer of lumber or plywood with a single manufacturing facility in a town with population less than 10,000. HUMANK equals 1 if the single-facility manufacturer is located in a city with population of over 10,000 people.

The coefficients on these variables assumed unanticipated negative signs when they were added to the regression for overbids. Apparently, collinearity of HUMANK and MILLTOWN with other explanatory variables and the paucity of timber volume on sales flagged by the HUMANK and MILLTOWN variables has prevented identification of independent human capital and implicit contract effects; the standard errors of the coefficients on HUMANK and MILLTOWN were at least as large as the coefficient estimates.

On the whole, these results are consistent with the explanation that timber buyers overbid on timber contracts in a gamble to avoid exit from the industry. Firms in subregions with the greatest need to disinvest of excess capacity tended to bid the most for timber contracts. Firms that could use bankruptcy laws to truncate their losses if timber conversion values turned downward made higher bids.

Patterns in Timber Volume Shares

Large firms with a high degree of wood self-sufficiency were relatively restrained in the timber auctions, winning sales at lower prices, on average, than other firms. The restraint exhibited by large firms also appears in the pattern of changes in timber volume shares. Large wood-owning firms generally reduced their share of coastal USFS timber purchased during the period of the largest overbids, 1979–81.

Table 3-2 presents further information on firms that purchased at least 0.3 percent of the douglas-fir, hem-fir timber volume sold in the USFS Coastal Region in 1975–78. The entries show that the group of firms with a large share of USFS sales in 1975–78, as a whole, made

TABLE 3-2

Shares of Timber Volume Purchased by Large Firms (percent of sales)

Firm Name	Share in 1975–78	Share in 1979–81	Change
Roseburg Lumber[a]	4.3	5.7	1.4
Williamette Industries[b]	3.4	2.4	−1.0
Champion International[b]	3.4	3.1	−0.3
Boise Cascade[b]	3.0	1.9	−1.1
Publishers Paper	3.0	2.6	−0.4
Southwest Forest Industries	2.5	2.4	−0.1
Bohemia[a]	2.3	2.5	0.2
Pope & Talbot	1.9	2.8	0.9
Crown Zellerbach[b]	1.5	0.8	−0.7
Medford Resources[a]	0.9	1.6	1.2
Seaboard Lumber[a]	0.9	1.2	0.3
Mt. Adams Veneer	0.8	0.7	−0.1
Louisiana Pacific[b]	0.7	0.4	−0.3
International Paper[b]	0.7	0.1	−0.6
Freres[a]	0.6	0.1	−0.5
Georgia-Pacific[b]	0.4	1.2	0.8
Simpson Timber	0.3	0.3	0.0
Self-sufficient subgroup	13.1	9.9	−4.2
Total	30.6	29.8	−0.8

[a] Firm qualified for minimum buyout rate on all sales returned to USFS.

[b] Firm estimated to be at least 25 percent wood self-sufficient as in the construction of the NOT LGOWN variable.

Source: Calculations by the author. Shares of total douglas-fir, hem-fir timber volume sold on USFS Westside Region 6 forests in the given fiscal years were calculated from the individual sales records in the Report of Timber Sales data base. The minimum buyout rate data were extracted from Regional Forester's Buyout Determination Summary records provided by USFS Region 6.

only a moderate reduction in purchased volume during the period of the largest overbids. However, six of the seven firms that were identified as at least 25 percent self-sufficient in timber reduced their share of volume purchased, and the wood self-sufficient subgroup reduced purchases by roughly one-fourth between 1975 and 1978 and between 1979 and 1981.

The behavior of Roseburg Lumber is somewhat anomalous. Roseburg Lumber was not included in the self-sufficient subgroup because no numerical estimate of Roseburg's degree of self-sufficiency was available in O'Laughlin and Ellefson (1982). However, the privately held firm is reported to have substantial timber land holdings. Roseburg Lumber was the largest single purchaser of USFS timber in the Coastal Region, and Roseburg increased its share of timber sold from 4.3 percent in 1975–78 to 5.7 percent in 1979–81. Roseburg is one of the firms that was eligible for the minimum buyout rates on all sales returned to the USFS, indicating that the firm would have been insolvent if the timber contracts had been enforced.

4

Psychology of the Market

This chapter discusses the psychology of the timber market during the period of highest overbids, 1979 through 1981. Specific consideration is given to the possibility that decisions of the timber buyers were quasirational, in the sense that the buyers chose actions that fitted their beliefs, but they held false beliefs.[1] Although the buyers' beliefs about future economic conditions cannot be known exactly, some clues to the way they made predictions can be culled from their testimony before Congress. Thus timber buyers' approach to forecasting is described on the basis of this testimony and of the properties of forecasting models that appear to have influenced their expectations.

Two kinds of long-run forecasts were widely cited by timber buyers: forecasts of the trend in new housing construction and forecasts of how product prices would change under the anticipated conditions of strong product demand and declining timber inventories. Almost invariably, timber buyers who cited the first mentioned that the high forecasts were based on anticipated demographic changes. With regard to product prices, the predicted decline in the inventory of timber available for sale was described as an impending "timber shortage." This chapter describes aspects of the long-run housing and "timber shortage" forecasts that made the strongest impressions on timber buyers, and it identifies a number of misconceptions about how the economic data should be interpreted. The principles of cognitive dissonance and budget maximization by government agencies are used to explain why the misconceptions developed.

Beliefs of Timber Buyers

We Live in the Long Run

The testimony of timber buyers suggests that government forecasts of long-run trends in the housing and forests products markets were a particularly strong influence on expectations about future timber values. Despite Keynes' admonition that all of us are dead in the long run, timber buyers assumed that they would be living in the long run; they assumed that the long-run forecasts were relevant in assessing the prospective profitability of a timber contract. More specifically, some timber buyers assumed that predictions of housing starts and lumber prices for the decade of the 1980s as a whole could reasonably be used for the medium-term (e.g., three years) horizons of the timber contracts.

Sometimes it is indeed reasonable to interpolate forecasts of the ten-year average of an economic variable to a higher frequency. Whether interpolation is prudent depends on the predictability of deviations from the ten-year trend. If cyclical deviations from the trend dampen down quickly, then the best projection of future cyclical deviations will be zero, and the best projection will be the trend projection.

Several timber buyers indicated that they believed in the existence of a "short cycle" in lumber prices. They indicated that their 1979–81 bids were based on the assumption that the downturn in lumber prices and demand would be of short duration because previous downturns had been short. For example, A. A. Emmerson said, "When lumber markets began to decline in 1979, we anticipated the usual short cycle and a renewal of markets within 6 to 12 months."[2] Barbara Webb cited the shift in Federal Reserve policies as the primary cause of a deviation from the usual short cycle: "We were against contract relief when we believed the recession would be of short duration, as they had been in the past. However it was not. Federal Reserve policies and high interest rates changed the rules of the game."[3]

Baby Boomers Would Create Record Housing Demand

It was widely believed that record single-unit housing demand would be created by the aging of the baby-boom generation. M. J. Kuehne recounted,

"The decade of the 1980's will be the golden age of single-family housing. As the baby boom of post–World War II outgrows condos and apartments, the United States will average over 2 million housing starts a year in the decade of the 1980's. The demographics of the population are such that the 1980's will see the highest level of housing starts in our history." These were the forecasts of business and Government economists that rang loud and clear in 1978 and 1979.[4]

Timber buyers were led to believe that total housing starts in the 1980s would be higher than ever before and that an unusually large proportion of the total would be single-family houses.

The pickup in the demographic demand for housing was widely cited. For example, Lynn Newbry said that bids were influenced by the fact that "there was demographic information coming from the Department of Housing and Urban Affairs indicating a need for two million housing starts per year during the decade of the eighties."[5] The major western timber industry associations jointly stated, "Government and reputable private economists foresaw a continuation of high inflation, moderate mortgage interest rates, and the entry of the post–World War II baby boom generation into its prime home-buying years."[6] The demographic demand aspect of the housing forecasts also was displayed prominently in an NFPA pamphlet publicizing the USFS timber assessment forecasts and was frequently discussed in DRI's FORSIM Review.[7]

A Timber Shortage Was Impending

In the late 1970s, the USFS and various state-sponsored commissions produced reports that suggested that forest product prices would increase much more quickly than the prices in general in the 1980s unless public timber harvest levels in the Pacific Northwest were drastically increased. These publications focused on estimating the historical and projected future path of the aggregate (public plus private) stock of mature timber at the prevailing levels of public and private timber management intensity. Projected public timber harvest levels were affected by projected growth rates for the timber stock. Given the expected low levels of public harvests, product prices were expected to have to appreciate quickly in order to bring forth enough private timber supply to meet the aggregate demand for timber.

The aggregate stock of prime timber in the Pacific Northwest had decreased significantly in the 1960s and 1970s as private timber owners harvested many of their old-growth timber stands. A timber stand is economically "mature" if the stand's anticipated biological growth rate, net of mortality from disease, fire, and other natural disasters, has slowed enough to make current harvest most profitable. On private lands, old-growth timber stands tended to be harvested before younger stands because the older trees had lower net biological growth rates than the younger trees. A timber supply "shortage" was predicted because, once the old-growth timber had been removed, the trees in the remaining inventory were expected to be growing quickly enough to warrant postponement of harvest. However, if product prices accelerated rapidly enough, the relatively immature trees would be harvested.

USDA forecasts of an impending timber shortage were widely cited as a cause of the overbidding. Craig (1982) cited the 1979 timber assessment projection as a contributor to the overbidding. He specifically cited the projection that the tight-supply, strong-demand conditions would cause deflated softwood lumber prices to rise 3.6 percent per anum on average between 1976 and 1990.[8] Hampton and Wood (1982) noted that the message of the 1979 timber assessment, that prices would rise unless planned public harvest levels were drastically increased, became common knowledge to the industry through NFPA (1980) and through congressional hearings on the Cooperative Forestry Assistance Act of 1978. John Davis, the general manager for one of the largest western timber buyers, described his interpretation of the timber assessment message in the following way:

> Government economists predicted moderate mortgage interest rates and a housing boom in the decade of the 1980's. Since Government itself controlled the amount of timber put up for sale each year and gave no sign it planned to increase the timber sale volume to match its predictions for increased demand for lumber and plywood, the result was to drive the prices bid to unrealistically high levels.[9]

A spokesman for Roseburg Lumber suggested that timber buyers did not recognize that the timber "shortage" predicted by the USFS was illusory until after they had acted on the projections: "The predicament of the Western Wood Products Industry was fostered by federal policies and U.S. Forest Service publications that created an illusion of a potential timber shortage. These policies constrained the supply made available, while predicting growing demand and high levels of inflation."[10] On the whole, the timber buyers' testimony to Congress suggests that the Forest Service's prediction that an impending timber shortage would cause an escalation in product prices was quite influential.

The USFS was not the only one predicting a rapid escalation in product prices in the 1980s. For example, similar predictions of growing product demand, tight timber supply, and product price escalation were made in the April 1978 issue of DRI's FORSIM Review. FORSIM argued that the declining inventory of coastal timber would create a steeper product supply curve for the U.S. wood products industry as a whole, that strong demand for wood products would be realized through 1985, and that the movement up the steep supply curve would result in a substantial increase in the price of douglas-fir 2 × 4's between 1977 and 1985.

Forest Service Projections

An Overview of the USFS Projection Methodology

The 1979 timber assessment predicted that the all-softwood-lumber Producer Price Index (PPI), deflated by the all-commodities PPI, would increase at a 2.8 percent annual rate over the period 1976–90. Deflated Coastal Region lumber prices were predicted to increase more quickly than national aggregate lumber prices. As just discussed, many timber buyers thought that long-run forecasts of housing starts were relevant because cyclical deviations were short, that the trend level of single-unit housing starts would be quite high because of demographic factors, and that a timber supply shortage in the Pacific Northwest would cause product prices to be high in the presence of the strong demand conditions. Since the timber assessment program of the USFS helped foster the beliefs in a demographic boost to housing starts and in a timber supply shortage, it will be useful to review how the USFS developed the timber assessment projections.

The 1979 timber assessment projections were derived in a two-step procedure. In the first step, base projections of quantity flows and prices for U.S. lumber, plywood, and other forest products were made. The base projections entered as exogenous variables in the Timber Assessment Market Model (TAMM) of Adams and Haynes (1980). In the second step, TAMM was solved to find implied product and timber prices.

The TAMM Model

In the TAMM terminology, a model is a "market" model if it provides estimates of prices and quantities by simulation of a competitive equilibrium. "Quasi-spatial" models disaggregate supply on a regional basis but explain product flows from each given supply region to only one demand region, so production and distribution decisions are not at all separable. Fully "spatial" models incorporate the spatial juxtaposition of production regions and consumption markets in an essential way by introducing separability in production and distri-bution decisions; delivered prices in consumption regions are depend-ent on the Free-on-board (FOB) mill prices of the various producers and on transportation costs.

TAMM is a spatial market model that is estimated and simulated with annual data. The TAMM model has been used primarily in conjunction with the "gap" analysis of the USFS timber assessments. In TAMM, the base projections of product prices and quantities are interpreted as indicating the rate at which product demand schedules will shift outward. The gap terminology was used to denote that there would be a disparity in the rate at which the demand and supply schedules shifted outward, since the inventory of mature timber was expected to increase more slowly than the nonprice determinants of demand. TAMM was supposed to determine the magnitude of the price increases necessary to equate effective demand and supply. The aggregates of the endogenous equilibrium regional prices and quantities in TAMM generally deviated from those used in the base projections.

The core of the TAMM model is a set of linear demand and supply equations for the product and stumpage markets by consumption and production regions. Market shares are determined implicitly. The TAMM simulation model comprises this system of linear equations at given values of the coefficients, with material-balance-type constraints, and with the assumption that the endogenous variables are those that satisfy the "spatial equilibrium solution" to this demand and supply system. The spatial equilibrium solution is that set of product market prices and quantities that maximizes the sum of consumer and producer surplus subject to the transportation cost and material-balance constraints. Since the solution is nonanalytic, it is identified computationally by a search algorithm. This algorithm exploits the property of the competitive equilibrium that at such an equilibrium a price-taking firm (region) could not perturb its production plans (aggregate level or distribution of shipments) in any way that increases profits.

In determining the magnitude of the product price increases necessary to equate effective product demand and supply, TAMM relied heavily on the coefficients in the product supply equations. If product supply was relatively unresponsive to changes in the price of the product itself, large price increases would be necessary to boost effective supply enough to meet an upward shift in demand.

Forest Service Housing Start Forecasts

TAMM's base projections of the consumption region quantity flows were based on the national aggregate end-use demand forecasts of the 1979 timber assessment. The end-use demand categories were similar to those in the model in Chapter 2. The new housing construction category of end-use demand is quantitatively most important and received the most attention from timber buyers.

Many analysts of long-run trends in housing construction, including the USFS, make use of an inventory identity that partitions the "demand" for new housing into three components: household formations, additional vacant units, and lost units. The starting point of the inventory identity is the constraint that the end-of-year stock of habitable houses must equal the beginning-of-year stock of habitable houses plus new units constructed, but net of losses by demolition and other forms of attrition. By inverting the constraint, one can see that the number of new units constructed equals the change in the habitable stock, net of losses to the stock. Some units in the habitable stock are held vacant; changes in the habitable stock are accompanied by changes in either the stock of occupied units or the stock of vacant units. Since each occupied unit is a household, these relations imply that each unit of new construction is accompanied by a household formation, an additional vacant unit, or the loss of a unit from the habitable stock.

Table 4-1 presents the USFS 1979 timber assessment projections for the components of the inventory identity, along with the historical data included in the publication. The USFS projected that the pace of housing construction would be 2.6 million total units per annum in the 1980s. This projection was based on household formations of 1.57 million units, additional vacancies of 0.19 million units, and net losses of 0.76 million units. The USFS 1979 housing start forecast was one of the most optimistic of those made in the late 1970s, but many analysts were also predicting that total starts would exceed 2 million units per year in the 1980s.

The USFS adopted the common assumption that the size and age distribution of the resident population of the United States are the most important long-run determinants of national household formation. Age is highly correlated with determinants of an individual's willingness to leave an existing household to form a new household. For example, age is highly correlated with income, emotional independence from parents, and marital status.

Projections of U.S. population by age class were translated into household formations by applying projected rates of household headship by age class. The household headship rate for an age class is the number of heads of household in that age class per persons in that age class.

TABLE 4-1

Inventory Changes Accompanying New Construction (thousands per annum)

Period	Housing Starts	=	Household Formations	+	Vacant Units	+	Lost Units	+	Other
1920–29	803		557		239		8		—
1930–39	365		496		−23		−108		—
1940–49	809		800		81		−72		—
1950–59	1522		1005		228		267		22
1960–69	1648		1039		−23		591		41
1970–77	2145		1532		120		415		78
Projection									
1980–89	2590		1570		190		760		70

Source: Table 3-3 of U.S. Department of Agriculture (1982).

The prediction of secular and cyclical movements in the headship rates is the most difficult part of forecasting household formation. Errors in predicting population by age class account for only a small portion of most analysts' errors in predicting household formation. Population projections are most difficult for the younger age classes, in which fertility and infant mortality rates are relevant, but people in the youngest age classes tend not to be household heads.

As shown in Figure 4-1, the distribution of headship rates across age classes has been relatively stable over time. In each decade shown, headship rates rose steeply at the younger ages and then increased at a relatively uniform rate. Between 1950 and the late 1970s, there had been a secular increase in the distribution of headship rates: The rate for each age class shifted upward. The USFS predicted that the upward shift in the distribution would continue, as higher headship rates were fostered by sociological factors and increasing per capita disposable income in the United States.

Although change in the number of occupied units (household formations) is the largest component of the long-run effective demand for additions to the housing stock, vacancy change is nonnegligible. Vacancies are classified as either frictional or nonfrictional. Frictional vacancies include units for sale and units for rent. Nonfrictional vacancies include migratory units, seasonal units, units held for occasional use, and miscellaneous. Since the frictional vacancy rate had been relatively stable over the preceding decades, the USFS assumed that the frictional vacancy rate for the 1980s would equal the observed 3.5 percent frictional vacancy rate of 1960 and 1970.[11] The USFS assumed that the nonfrictional vacancy rate would rise from 3.8 percent in 1977 to 5.5 percent by 1990.

The projected increases in the nonfrictional vacancy rate were based on high expectations for the second-home market. A second home was assumed to be a normal good that is jointly consumed with another normal good, leisure time. The increase in real incomes and the development of an older population with more leisure time were expected to increase the demand for second homes.

Besides new construction, net losses are the other source of change in the habitable housing stock. In the accounting framework of the *Annual Housing Survey*, important distinctions are made between types of losses. Permanent losses can never return to the inventory because they have been demolished by people, have been destroyed

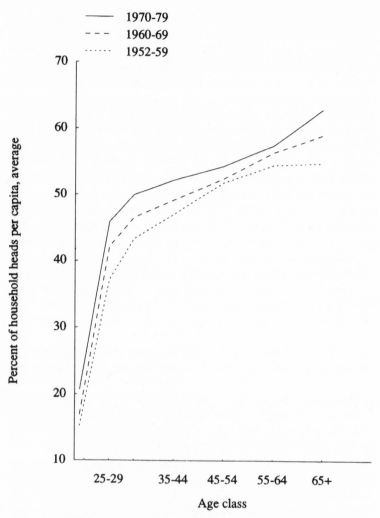

FIGURE 4–1. Household headship rates by age.

by natural disaster, or have otherwise been irretrievably lost.
Retrievable losses consist primarily of standing but uninhabitable
units such as those condemned for health and safety violations,
converted from many to fewer units, or converted from residential to
nonresidential use. Retrievable losses that do end up moving back

into the stock because they have been rehabilitated or reconverted join units such as original conversions from nonresidential to residential use in the tally of "unspecified units—net additions." Net losses are current permanent and retrievable losses less net additions.

Analysts of trends in net losses often refer to net losses as the "replacement demand for housing." In thinking about the secular growth path of the housing stock, conceiving of net losses as a form of replacement demand is appropriate. There would be no distinction between net losses and replacements if all losses were permanent, if there were no additions or losses from conversions and rehabilitations, and if additions from new construction always exceeded permanent losses. In fact, as the total housing stock grew from about 30 million units in 1930 to almost 90 million units in 1980, new construction did exceed net losses in each of the intervening decades. Conversion and rehabilitation activity had little net effect over the fifty-year span between 1930 and 1980, but there were wide swings in conversion and rehabilitation activities between the decades.

Quantitatively, the net loss category is very important. As shown in Table 4-1, net losses were expected to add 0.76 million units per year in the 1980s to the effective demand for new housing. Household formation was expected to add only about twice as much as net losses. The USFS cited the growing number of older units, the need to replace energy-inefficient houses, increases in per capita income, and a growing proportion of mobile homes with short life spans as causes of the anticipated increase in net losses.

The USFS housing projections were apportioned across types of units because the usage of lumber per dwelling unit differs markedly among single-unit structures, multiunit structures, and mobile homes. The USFS projected that single-unit production would be 1.68 million units per annum in the 1980s, 65 percent of the projected total unit production. The single-unit share projection assumed that the single-unit occupancy rates by age class that prevailed in the mid-1970s would continue to hold in the projection period. As in the distribution of household headship rates, the single-unit occupancy rates rise steeply at younger ages and then decrease gradually after about the age of 50 (Figure 4-2). The single-unit share of housing production was predicted to be high in the 1980s as the baby-boom generation moved into those age classes that traditionally were regarded as "the prime home-buying years."

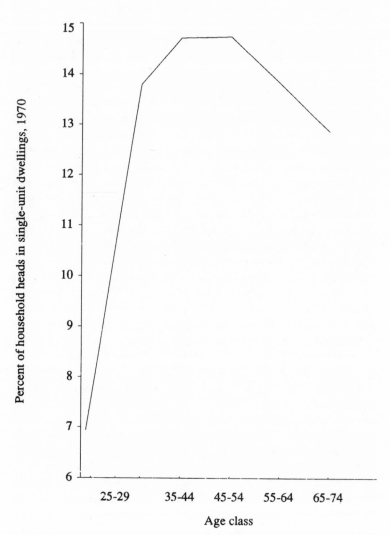

FIGURE 4–2. Single-unit share by age of household head.

Misconceptions

The belief that a substantial escalation in coastal lumber prices was likely over the term of a typical timber contract was fostered by several misconceptions. As just discussed, timber buyers thought that long-run forecasts of housing construction and lumber prices were relevant because cyclical deviations were short, that the trend level of single-unit housing construction would be quite high because of demographic factors, and that a timber supply "shortage" in the Pacific Northwest would cause product prices to accelerate, given the strong demand conditions. Each of these supporting arguments for high timber value projections relied on a misconception.

Living in the Short Run

The long-run forecasts should not have affected timber buyers' estimates of timber contract values because a long time is needed for housing construction and lumber prices to return to trend, once a cyclical downturn has begun. Furthermore, large shocks that move housing construction and lumber prices away from trend are common. Timber buyers were mistaken in believing in the existence of a "short cycle."

The nonexistence of the short cycle can be seen in the properties of the model introduced in Chapter 2. In the context of the model, a relevant short cycle would be the property that projections of timber conversion values twelve quarters ahead are determined almost exclusively by the projections of trends in end-use demands for lumber. However, projections of trends in end-use demands for lumber have little influence on the projections of timber conversion values twelve quarters ahead.

For example, let us consider two alternative simulations of the model. The first simulation uses the baseline forecast of the trend in housing construction, as in Chapter 2.[12] The baseline forecast assumes that the trend in total conventional housing construction, single-units plus multiunits, is about 2 million per year, with single-unit construction accounting for about 60 percent of the total. The second simulation uses the USFS forecast for the decade of the 1980s, interpolated uniformly to the quarterly level. The USFS forecast put the trend in total conventional housing construction at $2\frac{1}{4}$ million units per year, with single-unit construction accounting for about three-fourths of the total. When the model is simulated from the first quarter of 1978 to the third quarter of 1981, the average difference between the two alternative projections of twelve-quarter-ahead timber values is only about $1/MBF,LT. The difference between the estimates of future timber values is less than 1 percent of the average overbid on timber contracts during the 1978–81 period.

The model's projection of future timber values is relatively unresponsive to changes in the housing construction trend because, for many variables in the system, deviations from trend are quite predictable at the twelve-quarter horizon. For example, when simulated with data through the fourth quarter of 1980, the model predicts that total housing construction in the fourth quarter of 1983 will be one-third of a million units below trend.

The long-run and short-run properties of the model are very different. The short-run multiplier of trend housing construction on timber conversion values is small, but the long-run multiplier of trend housing construction on timber conversion values is relatively large. For example, at the 1980:4 level of manufacturing and logging costs, the total multiplier for the impact of coastal new orders on timber conversion value is $86/MBF, LT per billion board feet of annualized new orders. At the 1980:4 values of the coefficients that translate regional housing starts, by type of unit, into coastal lumber orders, each million units of national single-unit construction adds $1\frac{3}{4}$ BBF to coastal orders, each million units of multiunit construction adds $\frac{3}{4}$ BBF, and each million units of mobile homes adds slightly more than $\frac{1}{2}$ BBF. Thus a permanent increase in national housing construction from the baseline specification, which has total conventional starts at 2 million units and a moderate single-unit share, to the USFS projection, which has total conventional starts at $2\frac{1}{4}$ million units and a large single-unit share, would alter the long-run prediction of timber contract values by $56/MBF, LT.

Long-run housing forecasts are relevant in the long run, but not in the short run. Timber buyers' belief that deviations from trend were short was ill founded. The kind of short cycle that would justify using long-run forecasts of housing starts to project timber values did not exist.

Baby Boomers and Housing Demand

As noted in the preceding, forecasts that indicated the 1980s would be the golden age of single-family housing as the baby-boom generation outgrew condos and apartments rang loud and clear in the minds of timber buyers. The idea that the aging of the baby-boom generation was likely to support a high level of single-unit housing construction was misconceived. First, the link between household formations and housing construction is not tight enough to base a housing construction forecast almost exclusively on household formations. Second, by the end of the 1970s it was becoming clear that barriers to housing affordability were going to reduce the demand for single-unit housing significantly. While it was true that the baby-boom generation would develop a growing preference for housing other than condos and apartments at constant prices, the cost of detached single-unit housing was likely to rise enough to crowd out much of this potential demand.

NET LOSSES CAN SWAMP HOUSEHOLD FORMATIONS

Changes in the pace of net losses to the housing stock can outweigh the effect of household formations on housing construction. Within the course of a decade, the housing stock is too fungible, too capable of being adapted to its best use, for the pace of housing construction to be driven exclusively by household formations. In a decade when household formations significantly add to the demand for housing, conversion and alteration losses from the housing stock are likely to be low, partially relieving the need to meet the increased demand through new construction.

Furthermore, it is much more difficult to predict net losses to the housing stock than it is to predict household formations. Thus differences between long-run housing start forecasts tend to be largely attributable to different projections of net losses. While timber buyers frequently discussed demographic factors in their congressional testimony on timber contract modification, they appeared to be unaware of the importance of the net loss component. Therefore, timber buyers appear to have overreacted to predicted trends in household formation; more critical examination of the net loss projections by them would have been prudent.

The importance of the net loss component can be seen in a comparison of the USDA (1982) forecast for the decade of the 1980s to the realized components of inventory change in the early 1980s. As displayed in Table 4-1, the USDA predicted 1.57 million household formations, 0.19 million additional vacant units, 0.76 million net losses, and 0.07 million other additions in the 1980s. In 1980–83 there actually were 1.27 million household formations, 0.23 million additional vacant units, and 0.02 million net losses.[13] Thus net losses dominated the prediction error of the interpolated USFS long-run forecast.

A COHORT EFFECT IN SINGLE-UNIT HOUSING SHARES

When interpolated, the USDA (1982) forecast leads to a large overestimate of the single-unit proportion of new construction. The predicted single-unit share of 65 percent of total construction, including mobile homes, was much higher than the actual 1980–83 single-unit share of 54 percent. Much of this prediction error is attributable to the inappropriate use of the age of household heads as a correlate with single-unit occurrence rates. There is a substantial "cohort effect" in single-unit occurrence rates that makes this correlation change substantially over time.

In this context, a cohort effect is the tendency of a group initially occupying single-unit housing to continue to occupy single-unit housing as the group ages. Theoretically, a cohort effect can arise because the initial occupants grow more wealthy as housing prices appreciate and can use the capital gains on one house to buy another. Later entrants into the market for single-unit houses do not have these capital gains to use, and they consume less housing because they are less wealthy.

Although it is unclear whether the wealth effect is the best theoretical justification for the cohort effect, it is clear empirically that the cohort effect exists. The cohort effect appears as a twisting over time of the distribution of single-unit shares by age of household head (Figure 4-3). Unlike the distribution of household headship rates (Figure 4-1), younger age classes have tended to lose single-unit share as older age classes have increased share.

For example, 18- to 24-year-old household heads in 1960 had a much higher 18–24 occurrence rate (9.5 percent) than 18- to 24-year-

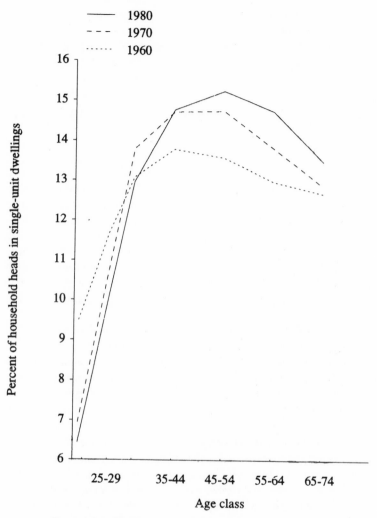

FIGURE 4-3. Single-unit share by age of household head.

olds in 1980 (6.5 percent). As the bulk of the group that was 18 to 24 years of age in 1960 moved into the 30–34 age class in 1970, the single-unit share for the 30–34 age class increased at the expense of people in younger age classes. Furthermore, when the group that was 18 to 24 years of age in 1960 moved into the 35–44 age class in 1980, the single-unit share for the 35–44 age class increased at the expense of people in younger age classes.

The fact that the baby-boom generation was moving into the mid-life age classes in the 1980s was not a good reason for expecting an increase in effective demand for single-unit housing. Single-unit share by age class was tending to shift down as the baby-boom generation entered older age classes.

Underestimates of Price Elasticities

As noted previously, the USFS predicted that the price of wood products would rapidly escalate in the 1980s as a boom in residential construction created a sharp upward movement along inelastic aggregate lumber and plywood supply curves. This potential development was described as a timber shortage because a declining inventory of mature timber was expected to make the product supply curves more inelastic. In retrospect, it is clear that the degree of elasticity in product supply was underestimated; the econometric estimators of the parameters determining product supply elasticity were biased downward.

As noted earlier, the USFS justified its assertion than an escalation in product prices was likely by referring to the TAMM model of Adams and Haynes (1980). The TAMM lumber supply equation was estimated in a "margin" form, with the excess of lumber price over manufacturing, logging, and timber costs being entered as a single variable. The TAMM lumber supply equation implied that the partial elasticity of coastal lumber supply with respect to deflated product price was 0.44.[14] This elasticity implies that a 1 percent increase in coastal lumber orders increases the ratio of coastal lumber price to the general price level by more than 2 percent, other things being equal.

A mismeasurement of timber prices biased the Adams and Haynes (1980) estimator of product supply elasticity downward, contributing to the overprediction of how much prices would increase in the presence of high levels of end-use demand. In a follow-up report to the 1979 timber assessment, Adams and Haynes noted that they originally overestimated timber costs in the Coastal Region by using historical timber price data that pertained only to national forest timber sales: "Since the average size and quality of National Forest timber is greater than the average for timber from all ownerships in the region, stumpage prices as reflected in historical data are too high."[15] The average size differential between logs in the USFS stumpage index and logs corresponding to the mill product price index causes the average overrun factor (mbf, log scale/mbf, lumber tally) for USFS logs to be smaller than that for all logs. Hence, stumpage costs are overstated if USFS overrun factors are used to convert stumpage costs to lumber tally. The quality differential implies that the mill price index has too little weight on product categories that bring high prices.

The noncomparability of the stumpage and mill price indices caused the TAMM (1980) margin variable to show a trend decrease over time and to be negative in the latter part of the sample. Supply was found to be relatively inelastic because the equation was forced to fit relatively high output levels to negative values.[16]

Another common misconception in empirical work on lumber supply elasticities is that the price paid for USFS timber cut can be treated as the variable cost of timber. However, since the USFS timber generally was purchased well in advance of the cutting date, the cut price is not analogous to the spot market price. When market conditions turn out to differ from what timber buyers anticipated at the time of contract origination, the cut price can diverge greatly from the spot market price. This source of error in measuring the variable cost of timber also can lead to a downward bias in estimators of lumber price elasticity.[17]

Development of the Misconceptions

Timber buyers did not forecast as if they were superrational agent econometricians who correctly interpreted available economic data. Three specific shortcomings in their approach to forecasting have been identified. First, contrary to what the timber buyers assumed, deviations from the trend in housing starts were predictable. Second, demographic factors alone were unlikely to create a boom in single-unit housing construction. Last, historical data on the price of federal timber was misinterpreted in econometric estimates of coastal lumber supply elasticity.

In trying to understand why these misconceptions developed, it will be useful to focus separately on the behavior of the timber buyers and the behavior of the USFS. Also, it will be useful to try to explain the behavior of each group in purposive terms, as a means to some end, even though it is possible that the misconceptions were simply mistakes and nothing more.

Timber buyers benefited from their mistaken beliefs in psychic terms: by believing in a housing boom and timber shortage, they could justify gambling on the timber contracts. The Forest Service stood to benefit from the specter of a housing boom and timber shortage in institutional terms—it used the 1979 timber assessment report to lobby Congress for a larger budget.

Cognitive Dissonance

Cognitive dissonance is a form of selection bias in the acquisition of beliefs. The cognitive dissonance principle asserts that, ceteris paribus, people are disposed to avoid beliefs that create negative emotions. Timber buyers' descriptions of how they approached forecasting support the interpretation that they were exhibiting cognitive dissonance.

As explained in Chapter 3, many timber buyers faced the choice of either purchasing federal timber or liquidating their mills. For some mill owners, purchasing the federal timber was preferred to liquidation over a wide range of expected timber conversion values. Bidding behavior was relatively insensitive to expectations about timber conversion values because bankruptcy could be used to truncate losses, and the required deposits were insensitive to the risk of default. At the high bid prices of 1979–81, these firms faced almost certain closure whether or not they purchased the federal timber. Mill owners sought to avoid the negative emotions associated with the thought of mill closure.

The testimony of the timber buyers suggests that many of them adhered to rules of thumb that they associated with avoiding mill closure. These rules of thumb stated upper and lower limits for the inventory of timber to be kept under contract, and inventory thresholds were defined as proportions of the firm's average annual production.

Expectations of timber conversion values could have affected timber buying decisions only if the expectations were formed before a rigid decision to purchase timber was made. The firms that adhered rigidly to the inventory limit rules of thumb inverted the temporal order necessary for expectations to affect decisions—these firms bought first, and then they calculated forecasts that would justify their bids. The cognitively dissonant firms framed the question of how they should develop expectations as a question of justification: Preferred forecasts of future timber values were those that would let them win enough sales to stay within the inventory limits.

For example, let us carefully consider the language the spokesman for the North West Timber Association used to describe why timber bids escalated so rapidly:

> Our membership is located in Western Oregon and Washington. They are all small businesses and are nearly 100 percent dependent upon the public agencies for their timber supply. Because they must buy all of their timber in public auctions, they must maintain competitive, efficient mills. There has been a constant upgrading of these mills which reflects heavy dollar investments. With these heavy investments it is imperative that a steady source of raw material is purchased out ahead. A very reasonable inventory of timber is 2 to $2\frac{1}{2}$ years' supply. As the inflation factors rose to double digit rates, these rates had to crank into the timber bids and compounded [*sic*] annually in order to buy the sale. Continued optimistic predictions by renowned economists also fed the flames of unprecedented bidding. Call it speculative bidding if you will. Most companies so heavily dependent upon the public timber considered it a matter of survival. They had to crank in all of the factors that they could anticipate to develop a bid value projection to fit the anticipated market some 2 to 3 years in the future.[18]

The last two sentences in this passage are quite revealing, especially the use of the word "could." These timber buyers did not frame the question of how conversion values should be projected as one of identifying all of the factors that they *should* anticipate. They framed the question as one of searching for forecasts that would justify bids high enough to win sales.

Other timber buyers made similar statements. For example, Fred Sohn said,

> The year of 1979 started in earnest the irrational bidding for public timber. We used every appraisal device imaginable attempting to justify the $400, $500, and $600 stumpage prices that were being bid. We could not find one, short of adding yearly inflation increments in the range of 10 to 12 percent to just get close to these numbers.[19]

Another explicitly stated that the government forecasts helped them justify the bidding behavior to themselves; the spokesman for Taylor Lumber Company explained that in 1980 they look at the government forecasts after facing "a very grim reality" and deciding to bid whatever was necessary to win the contracts:

> They faced the fact that several companies had to face at the same time, that there are basically two ways to go out of business in our industry. One is to have no timber to process, and the other is to have timber that may be too costly to process. Taylor decided that if it was going to stay in business, keep its 130 workers employed, and maintain some semblance of economic stability in the town of Sheridan, it would have to do whatever was necessary to secure a supply of timber. They looked at the Government housing projections. They looked at the Forest Service forecast of demand for lumber, and they decided to bid timber sales accordingly, as did their competitors. They didn't like bidding high prices and they didn't do it by choice, but they did it as the only alternative to shutting down permanently.[20]

Timber buyers who sought to avoid the specter of mill closure framed the question of how to forecast as one of finding forecasts that justified bids high enough to win sales.

Lobbying for a Larger Budget

The Forest Service holds the forest products industry hostage in the agency's battle for a larger budget.[21] The 1979 timber assessment report was a crucial weapon in this battle. The report warned Congress of an impending timber shortage and implied that increased expenditures on public timber management and research were the only effective way to increase the flow of timber from the national forests. The forest products industry supported the call for increased expenditures because the industry wanted the flow of timber from the national forests to be increased.

As a matter of policy, the USFS maintains a peculiar relationship between management intensity on USFS forests and the amount of timber offered for sale. The quantity of public timber offered depends on annual allowable sales figures determined in the USFS resource-planning process. The pattern of planned sale offerings is constrained by a policy of "nondeclining sustained yield." As usually interpreted, the nondeclining sustained yield policy implies that the planned sale offerings can never exceed the maximum level of cut that could be sustained in perpetuity. In turn, the maximum level of sustainable cut depends on the net biological growth rate of those trees on land deemed eligible for timber production.

The Forest Service's budget helps determine the actual level of sales offerings in two ways. First, the budget affects sale offering plans because the estimated net biological growth rates of USFS timber are a function of USFS management intensity, and USFS management intensity depends on its budget. Second, timber sales offerings generally are less than planned offerings in years when the Forest Service has not had enough spending authorization to administer the full sale program.

The foreword to the 1979 timber assessment report (USDA, 1982) summarizes its "analytical" conclusions the following way:

> Although there has been much progress, there is little likelihood of a timber surplus. The projections in this study show that our demands for timber are likely to grow rapidly. They also show that the supplies of timber available to meet these demands will increase, but more slowly. As a consequence, we face intensifying competition for timber and continuing increases in stumpage and timber product prices.

The foreword also notes that the outlook can be changed if the growing stock is managed more intensively or improvements are made in the utilization of the wood in the forests. Producing enough timber to meet the predicted domestic and export demands is set out as a goal for the USFS and private industry. The foreword concludes with the prescription, "Moving forward to achieve this goal will require large public and private investments in management, assistance, and research programs." This foreword clearly articulates the Forest Service position in lobbying for a larger budget.

5

Reform in the Aftermath of the Bailout

This chapter reviews how timber planning and sale procedures have changed since the late 1970s and presents proposals for further reform. Many of the conditions that fostered the 1979–81 overbidding still exist, and the proposed reforms aim to eliminate some of these conditions.

The overbidding period 1979–81 had four key features:

1. A disruption of public timber supply left the coastal lumber industry with excess capacity.
2. Inadequate deposits left the Forest Service exposed to great risk of timber contract defaults and encouraged those firms closest to insolvency to overbid the most.
3. The small-business set-aside program encouraged overbidding by tying timber set-aside volume shares in the post-1981 period to pre-1981 purchased volume shares.
4. USFS timber assessment projections that real product prices would sharply escalate in the 1980s made it easier for timber buyers to believe that a gamble on timber contracts was likely to pay off.

None of these problems has been fully resolved. Uncertainty about public timber supply continues to be sizable, leaving a high risk of another capacity imbalance. The Forest Service has reduced exposure to default risk, but a rapid escalation of overbidding by insolvent firms remains a distinct possibility. The set-aside program continues to foster a small-firm market structure, and another bout of overbidding to affect set-aside shares appears likely before the 1991 date of share redetermination. The 1989 timber assessment report

68

projects a sharp escalation of product prices in the 1990s without adequately warning readers of the fragility of the projection.

Most of the reforms proposed here concern the way timber sales are planned, the way timber sales are awarded, and the actual specifications of the timber contracts. A revision to the content of the timber assessment report also is proposed.

Timber Assessment Projections

Current State of Affairs

The draft 1989 timber assessment report (U.S. Department of Agriculture, 1989) is very similar to the 1979 timber assessment report (U.S. Department of Agriculture, 1982). Using basically the same methodology as was used in the 1979 assessment, the 1989 assessment projects a rapid escalation of forest product prices. The message of both reports is clear: Additional funding of those Forest Service programs that increase timber production would help stem an undesirable acceleration of product prices.

The latest report projects that in the next decade, softwood lumber prices will increase about 2 percentage points per year more quickly than overall producer prices, giving the projected path of lumber prices an upward profile resembling that projected in the 1979 report. The impending escalation of product prices is expected to occur because growth of timber demand would outpace growth of timber supply at current prices. The Forest Service states that the price increases are fairly certain to occur because "futures analysis...has shown that these price increases can be expected to occur under a wide range of possible supply and demand conditions."[1] Because rising timber prices are expected to have an adverse effect on the environment and general economic conditions, the report concludes that "the primary implication of the Assessment for timber programs is to respond to the projected demand-supply situation with options for slowing the rate of increase in timber prices."[2] Acceleration of public timber harvests is offered as one of the options for slowing timber prices, and the report notes that such a harvest acceleration would require expansion of existing Forest Service programs.

As for the methodology used for the 1989 timber assessment

projections, once again the housing start forecast relies heavily on demographic factors, and the TAMM model is used to infer how the projected path of end-use demand and timber supply would affect product prices. An acceleration of end-use demand for lumber is expected to occur, partially because the single-unit share of new housing construction is expected to be high. Again, high expectations for the single-unit share are based on the misconception that the aging of the baby-boom generation will boost effective demand for single-unit housing:

> Single-family houses are typically occupied by households whose heads are in the middle age classes, while occupancy of units in multifamily buildings and mobile homes is highest among households headed by younger and older persons. As a result of prospective shifts in the age distribution of the population, and the associated changes in household types and income, the numbers of conventional single-family units are projected to fluctuate but generally remain near 1.1 million through most of the projection period.[3]

As in the 1979 assessment, the relatively strong outlook for total housing starts is justified by a moderate pace of household formation and a sharp pickup in replacement of housing units.

Proposed Reforms

Inappropriate use of the timber assessment projections should be discouraged. Currently, the Forest Service's degree of confidence in the projections is vastly overstated, encouraging readers who do not understand the political and institutional context of the projection process to believe the Forest Service's claim that "these price increases can be expected to occur under a wide range of possible supply and demand conditions. Consequently, they are fairly certain to occur."[4] In fact, the Forest Service price projections are subject to a great deal of uncertainty. The uncertainty about the projections should be quantified better in the timber assessment reports.

Currently, projection uncertainty is quantified only through examining how alternative assumptions for exogenous variables affect the projections of the TAMM model.[5] However, uncertainty about exogenous variables is only one of four important sources of uncertainty about the projections of an econometric model. The projections also are subject to model specification uncertainty, parameter estimate uncertainty, and residual uncertainty. Confidence intervals for the econometric model projections would widen considerably if these additional forms of uncertainty were incorporated.

Public Timber Supply

Current State of Affairs

Actual and potential fluctuations in public timber supply continue to plague the coastal region. In subregions where most firms are heavily dependent on federal timber, mill profitability continues to be affected greatly by fluctuations in public timber sale volumes. The volume of public timber sale offerings is subject to great uncertainty, and sale offering volumes have a relatively direct impact on mill profitability through timber prices. Making public timber sale volumes significantly more predictable would be relatively difficult, but the short-run impact of variations in public timber supply on mill profitability can be diminished.

Uncertainty about sale offering volumes is an inherent part of the timber-management-planning process. Timber management planning is a formal process in which competing interest groups have an opportunity to affect the way national resources are used. Some mechanism for resolving disputes about renewable resource management is essential. One way to reduce uncertainty about sale offering volumes is to shift the timing of the resolution of disputes forward in a lengthened process, giving potential timber buyers more time to adapt if land is taken away from the timber production use.

Timber management planning takes place at three levels: national, regional, and individual forest.[6] National planners develop the Resources Planning Act (RPA) assessment and the RPA program. Regional foresters develop regional guides that translate objectives from the RPA program into objectives for each forest in the region. Forest supervisors develop forest plans that include the plan from the regional guide as one of several alternatives.

The RPA assessment includes an inventory of renewable resources, an analysis of present and prospective future demand and supply situations, and an evaluation of how investments in resource management would affect future supply. The RPA assessment is to serve as the factual basis for the RPA program. The RPA program is a long-term strategic-planning document that displays planned levels of future timber sale offerings and other goals.

The RPA assessment program is completed on a ten-year cycle; an RPA program is established at the beginning of each decade. The RPA program displays timber sale schedules for several decade-long planning periods. Only the sale schedule for the first decade establishes an allowable sale quantity; sale schedules for other decades are shown to indicate whether a sale program is sustainable. The regional guides are a mechanism through which the RPA program influences individual forest plans. At any given time, forest plans are being developed for individual national forests, and the forest plans are scheduled for revision on a ten- to fifteen-year cycle.

The Forest Service submits budget proposals to Congress yearly, asking for funds to implement the programs displayed in the various planning documents. The actual level of timber sale offerings depends on both the proposed sale program and the amount of funding the Forest Service receives. Funding affects the pace of individual timber sale preparation. Planning a specific timber sale often takes as long as five years, and a long period of budget austerity can reduce the inventory of sales under preparation. Short periods of budget austerity temporarily slow the flow of sale offerings from the inventory of sales under preparation.[7] The planning process takes a long time because any given timber sale is relatively likely to be held up by litigation unless it conforms to a forest plan that meets the requirements of the RPA or conforms to an alternative, less comprehensive, land-use plan that documents the absence of adverse environmental impact. Short-term fluctuations in funding affect the flow of sale offerings because timber sale preparation activities such as appraisals require substantial financial resources.

The individual forest plans include a timber sale schedule that defines an allowable sale quantity. A base sale schedule must be considered in the forest plans. Under the base sale schedule, planned sales for a decade would not exceed the long-term sustained yield of the forest, given the current RPA program and regional guide. Departures from the base sale schedule can be adopted if, for example, "implementation of the corresponding base sale schedule would cause a substantial adverse impact upon a community in the economic area in which the forest is located."[8]

Uncertainty is inherent in the timber-management-planning process. At any time, development of an individual forest plan can be completed, potentially indicating a major reduction in the land area available for producing timber in that forest. Further uncertainty is introduced by the need to predict how the forest service will react to forest plans—regional foresters can and often do delay implementation of forest plans by withholding approval. Each year, sale offerings fluctuate with the degree of budget austerity. Each decade, prospective sale offering levels can be revised drastically when a new RPA program is adopted. From time to time, legislators and the courts introduce further uncertainty into the process by objecting to Forest Service plans or practices.

In mid-1989, there was a great deal of uncertainty about future sale offering levels in the coastal region. All Oregon and Washington timber sales by the USFS near suspected spotted owl habitat areas were under injunction, preventing most of the planned sales for fiscal year 1989 in Westside Region 6 from being finalized.[9] A draft of the 1990 RPA program, circulating for public comment on five possible final programs, indicated that softwood timber sale offerings in USFS Region 6 would drop from 5.2 BBF in 1987 to between 4.5 and 4.7 BBF in 1995.[10]

A reduction of 1990s timber sale offerings well below 4.5 BBF appeared to be a distinct possibility, because the spotted owl was being considered for listing as an endangered species. Public timber purchasers in the coastal region feared that listing of the spotted owl as an endangered species would lead to a major overhaul of the Forest Service's spotted owl management program. The draft 1990 RPA program sale offering levels are based on the existing spotted owl management program.

Currently, public timber sale volumes have a relatively direct impact on mill profitability because the inventory of outstanding timber contracts is relatively small. The inventory of outstanding timber contracts has diminished as typical contract term lengths were shortened in the aftermath of the bailout. With smaller inventories of timber under contract, timber purchasers are less able to offset temporary reductions in sale offerings by drawing down inventories.

Proposed Reforms

Timber management planning is to "provide, so far as feasible, an even flow of national forest timber in order to facilitate the stabilization of communities and opportunities for employment."[11] In practice, large year-to-year variations in sale offerings occur. Currently, the variations in sale offerings have a large short-run effect on the flow of timber from the forests. Timber management procedures should be reformed to reduce uncertainty about sale offerings and to break the short-run link between sale offerings and the flow of timber from the forests.

The timber-management-planning process is an essential mechanism for resolving disputes among competing interest groups about resource management. Uncertainty about timber sale levels, which stems from uncertainty about which group's interest will prevail, is inherent. However, uncertainty about sale offering levels could be reduced if the process of resolving disputes was started well before the timber was to be harvested, giving potential timber buyers more time to adapt to increased use of forest land for nontimber purposes. A timber planning process in which sales are conducted well in advance of expected harvest would produce a larger pool of outstanding contracts. By increasing the pool of outstanding timber contracts, the Forest Service could diminish the short-run impact of variations in sale offerings on mill profitability.[12]

Insolvency and Default Risk

Current State of Affairs

The Forest Service has reduced its exposure to default risk, but a rapid escalation of overbidding by insolvent firms remains a distinct possibility. Exposure to default risk has been reduced by increasing scrutiny of bidders' financial strength, shortening of contract term lengths, indexing of timber payment rates to product prices, and the requirement of midpoint payments and larger initial deposits. The possibility of insolvent firms engaging in a rapid escalation of overbidding remains significant, however, because the deposit and payment requirements still are too insensitive to the individual purchaser's risk of default.

Currently, the Forest Service uses a restricted form of "pay-as-you-cut" system in the Coastal Region. As in the 1979–81 period, timber buyers are required to maintain a payment balance with the USFS that might equal, for example, the expected payment due on timber to be cut in the following month. Unlike in the earlier period, midpoint payments now are required on all contracts with a term greater than one year. The midpoint payments are 25 percent of the bid value or 50 percent of the bid premium (excess of bid value over advertised value), whichever is greater. Furthermore, now species-specific timber payment rates generally are indexed to product prices through stumpage rate adjustment clauses.

The deposit system provides the Forest Service with security against more than one type of default. As in the pre-bailout period, timber contracts usually require a small performance bond that covers, for example, the cost of cleaning up after a harvest. The performance bond requirement was in place before the early 1980s because the most likely form of default appeared to be failure to perform activities that take place after harvest. After a harvest, the timber cannot serve as collateral that could be retained by the Forest Service. The 1979–81 overbidding episode heightened awareness of another form of default—failure to remove any timber from the sale area.

In the aftermath of the bailout, timber buyers have been required to make larger down payments. In the 1979–81 period, the typical down payment was 5 percent of the bid value. Now the down payment is at least 10 percent of the bid value. The down payment rate increases to 10 percent of the advertised value plus 20 percent of the bid premium on national forests where the average ratio of bid to advertised value has exceeded 1.6 in the previous fiscal year. Down payment requirements are highest for a firm that is in arrears to the USFS in the sense that the firm has defaulted a timber sale and not fully paid the damages. A firm in arrears to the USFS must make a down payment equal to 20 percent of the advertised value plus 40 percent of the bid premium.[13]

The provisions for higher down payments from firms in arrears and from firms in national forests with high overbid ratios increase the sensitivity of down payments to default risk. Furthermore, although timber contracts generally are awarded to the highest bidder, a contracting officer is not allowed to award the contract without affirming that the bidder is a responsible purchaser. Now the Forest Service follows the Federal Acquisition Regulations, which specify that a contracting officer must find that the firm has adequate financial resources to perform a contract.[14]

The new procedures for determining purchaser financial responsibility are a great improvement, but they do not eliminate enough default risk and they come at a high administrative cost. The procedures direct a contracting officer to request a financial ability analysis from a Forest Service staff accountant unless such an analysis has been completed within the preceding twelve months by a government agency.[15] If the bid value on the contract in question and other outstanding contracts exceeds $300,000, potential timber buyers are required to provide a timber portfolio gain/loss projection and a comprehensive set of financial statements that have been certified by a public accountant. The portfolio gain/loss projection shows anticipated gains and losses on outstanding timber contracts, as estimated by the bidder and critically reviewed by the Forest Service. If the portfolio projection shows that anticipated losses exceed either current working capital or net worth, bidders are required to submit a cash flow forecast. A contract is to be awarded only if a bidder's ability to meet the cash requirements of the sale can be established through this process.

A significant amount of default risk remains because rationing of high-risk firms takes place only at contract origination. A purchaser's financial condition and market conditions can change greatly over the course of a contract term. The timber portfolio gain/loss projection on which a financial responsibility finding is made can become obsolete quickly as market conditions change. For example, in 1980 the projected value of a douglas-fir timber contract fell to less than half of the projected value in 1979 (Figure 2-1), mirroring similarly large fluctuations in the spot value of the timber. Default risk increases as portfolio profitability deteriorates, but currently the Forest Service does not have an automatic mechanism for obtaining increased security when default risk increases.

Proposed Reforms

Firms with high risk of default need to be rationed out of the timber market, as is done currently by the financial ability analysis process.

Furthermore, this rationing mechanism has to be augmented by deposit requirements that vary with the Forest Service's exposure to default risk. Full payment of the bid premium at contract origination should be required, lessening the initial Forest Service exposure to loss through default. The bid premium deposit should be fully updated quarterly, on the basis of updated appraisals that evolve with prices in the product markets. Currently, the Forest Service updates timber portfolio profitability analyses quarterly in Region 6, so the basic data for conducting such quarterly updates of bid premium deposits are available.

Set-aside Program

Current State of Affairs

The small-business set-aside program continues to be administered, affecting the pattern of contract awards. Currently, in more than half the market areas in the Coastal Region small firms are guaranteed more than 60 percent of timber sales (Table 5-1). As explained in Chapter 3, set-aside shares are re-determined every five years. More frequent changes in set-aside shares occur only if there has been a structural change in the market area, such as a change in the size class of a firm or the discontinuance of operations by a firm.[16] Another bout of overbidding to affect set-aside shares in the next five-year period appears likely before the 1991 date of share re-determination.

Current guaranteed shares were determined at the beginning of fiscal year 1986, and most base shares remained at those established in 1981 under a special policy adopted because of the unusual events of 1981 to 1985.[17] When base shares are recomputed in 1991, an average of small-business purchasing share and harvesting share in 1986 to 1990 is to be used. Small firms have bid more aggressively than large firms in recent years, partly because the buyout regulations placed a limit on returned volume and left many large firms with substantial inventories of uncut federal timber. With purchase and harvest history available for three of the five years in the 1986–91 period, large firms were threatened with increases in the guaranteed small-firm share in most of the market areas in the Coastal Region (Table 5-1).

Partly in response to objections to the prospective upward

TABLE 5-1

Small-Business Shares in USFS Westside Region 6

Forest	Market Area	Base Share 1986–90	Actual Share 1986–88[a]	Difference
Deschutes	Deschutes	33	30	−3
Fremont	Klamath Basin	62	61	−1
	Lakeview	36	35	−1
G. Pinchot	North	64	76	12
	South	69	80	11
Mt. Baker	Mt. Baker	80	80	0
Snoqualmie	Snoqualmie	75	69	−6
Mt. Hood	East	80	80	0
	West	63	77	14
Okanogan	Okanogan	22	24	2
Olympic	Peninsula	61	76	15
	Quinault	71	80	9
Rogue River	Rogue River	64	66	2
Siskiyou	East	40	62	22
	West	79	80	1
Siuslaw	Hebo	64	80	14
	Mapleton	71	80	9
	Alsea-Walport	70	80	10
Umpqua	North	10	34	24
	South	45	44	−1
Wenatchee	Chelan	36	49	13
	Kittitas	46	52	6
	Naches-Tieton	34	44	10
Williamette	North	49	80	31
	Middle	75	74	−1
	South	53	57	4
Winema	Winema	48	45	−3

[a] Average of estimated small-business purchase and harvest shares for 10/1/85–9/30/88, fiscal years 1986–88.

Source: Correspondence with USFS Region 6, 14 August 1989.

ratcheting of small-firm guaranteed shares, in September 1987 the Forest Service proposed that Region 6 base shares be frozen pending complete review of the set-aside program in 1991. Despite several congressional hearings on the proposed changes to the set-aside program, the Forest Service has not made a final decision on the proposal to freeze base shares.[18] Given current policy, in 1990 large firms are likely to try to win back some of the eroded large-firm share before the share reductions are locked in for the 1991–96 period.

Any reforms to the set-aside program should preserve the program's established benefits while reducing the disruptive effects of the program. Secularly, the program disrupts the structure of the coastal lumber and plywood industry by protecting small firms. In regular cycles, the program disrupts bidding incentives by encouraging small and large firms to battle over the upward ratcheting of small-firm guaranteed shares. No beneficial effects of the program have ever been documented, but some advocates of the program claim that the atomistic market structure fostered by the program creates internal and external benefits.

A common argument is that the set-aside program creates a positive externality: Small firms provide more community stability than large firms because small firms are loyal to their community, whereas large firms are driven solely by the profit motive.[19] Another common argument is that the set-aside program creates a benefit internal to the market: An atomistic timber buyer market prevents collusion and increases the revenues of the federal government.[20] The SBA has stated that the current set-aside program is justified by the Small Business Act, which directed the SBA "to work with other agencies to insure that small business received its fair proportion of the total sales of Government property."[21] In the context of timber sales, the concept of a "fair" small-business share is too vague to be useful, but the arguments about internal and external economic benefits are precise enough to warrant study.

All the arguments presume that large firms would drive small firms out in the absence of the set-aside program. Some small firms have argued that large firms would act as predators. For example, the spokesman for Bennett Lumber Company argued that

> the Set-Aside Program is our lifeblood. It protects us from our large business neighbors who, from time-to-time, attempt to buy all the federal timber available for purchase. Because we do not have access to an alternative supply of timber, we cannot keep our mills operating unless we can buy consistently from the Forest Service. Without the Set-Aside Program, as sure as I am sitting here, we would be forced out of business any time a company such as Potlach or Weyerhauser decides to expand its operations.[22]

The real issue is whether a large firm such as Potlach or Weyerhauser should be able to force small firms out of business if the large firm is more efficient. The experience of the early 1980s suggests that an efficient adjustment of capacity to fluctuations in timber supply might require the exit of small firms that do not have either private timber or the financial resources to withstand temporary fluctuations in timber supply. Whether the set-aside program impedes efficient adjustment of capacity to fluctuations in timber supply is an important issue.

The spokesman for the North West Timber Association is among those who denied that the perceived impediment to efficient adjustment was a legitimate concern:

> Capacity of our industry will adjust in response to changing supply through free competition—the most efficient will survive, while the weak will fall by the way. We can deal with this environment so long as we are protected from the sheer financial magnitude of the giant corporations— the purpose of the SBA timber program.[23]

This rebuttal incorrectly presumes that financial strength should be omitted as a determinant of efficiency. However, a large-firm market structure might be more efficient exactly because large firms tend to have more substantial holdings of private timber and better financial resources for surviving fluctuations in public timber supply.

Not all SBA programs permanently impede the development of efficient market structure. An atomistic market structure may be efficient, but hard to realize in the absence of government intervention, if small firms are particularly vulnerable to predation when they first enter the market. After a small firm is well established, it should not be considered efficient unless it has the resources to survive future fluctuations in timber supply. Some SBA programs provide preferential treatment to firms only during a start-up period, implicitly recognizing that the small-firm–large-firm issue is similar to the infant industry problem of international trade. For example, the Minority Small Business and Capital Ownership Development Program of the SBA has a fixed program participation term, so firms receiving preferential treatment under this program are given only a limited time before they face the test of efficiency posed by an open market.[24]

Proposed Reforms

Like the SBA program for small minority firms, the timber set-aside program should have a fixed term of program participation. Correspondingly, the timber set-aside program should make determinations of how much preferential treatment to give specific firms on the basis of individual firm characteristics, not on the purchase and harvest history of the group of small firms.

Appendix: A Model for Projecting Coastal Timber Values

This appendix presents the model used to project coastal timber values. The documentation includes descriptions of identities and stochastic equations in the model and a listing of data sources. The organization of the appendix follows the model's recursive structure: The equations most proximate to the determination of the conversion value of timber, X, are presented first. The description of data set construction is presented last.

For definitions of variables appearing in model equations, the reader may wish to refer to the data description section (Data Set Construction and Sources). Most stochastic equations include lagged dependent variables; the lag polynomial for dependent variables is given on the right side of the equations, with lag operator (L) notation. The t subscript denotes time indexed at a quarterly frequency. The T subscript denotes time indexed at an annual frequency. See Mattey (1988) for a fuller description of the model.

Timber and Lumber Equations

No.	Dependent Variable	Equation
1	X_t	$= Z_t * \mathrm{MLC}_t \quad \text{for } X_t = P_t - \mathrm{MLC}_t - R_t^k$
2	$\Delta \log(\mathrm{MLC}_t)$	$= (1 - 2.05L + 1.59L^2 - 0.476L^3 - 0.001L^4)^{-1}$ $[-0.0000 + 0.0005\ D1_t + 0.0000\ D2_t + 0.0003D3_t$ $+ (-0.019 - 0.003L + 0.029L^2 + 0.017L^3 - 0.005L^4)\Pi_t]$
3	Z_t	$= (1 - 1.27L + 0.650L^2 - 0.232L^3 + 0.011L^4)^{-1}$ $[-0.686 + 0.128D1_t + 0.032D2_t - 0.029D3_t$ $+ (0.184 + 0.118L + 0.032L^2 - 0.079L^3 + 0.154L^4).001Q_t]$
4	Q_t	$= \left(\sum_i \gamma_{it} \mathrm{EUD}_{it} \right) + \mathrm{QRESID}_t$
5	γ_{it}	$= \sum_j \mathrm{MS}_{jt} \mathrm{UF}_{ijt} \mathrm{RSEUD}_{ijt} \quad i = 1,\ldots,6$
6	QRESID_t	$= (1 - 0.189L - 0.005L^2 - 0.026L^3 + 0.134L^4)^{-1}$ $[777.4 + 282.0D1_t - 232.5D2_t - 172.0D3_t - 3.02\mathrm{TREND}_t$ $+ (-118.7 - 93.0L + 196.0L^2 + 218.9L^3 - 541.5L^4)\mathrm{GNP}_t]$

End-use Equations

No.	Dependent Variable	Equation
7	EUD^c_{1t}	$= (1 - 0.741L + 0.382L^2 - 0.292L^3 + 0.094L^4)^{-1}$ $[-25.7 - 33.2D1_t + 96.6D2_t - 10.8D3_t$ $+ (-3129 + 6049L - 5328L^2 + 5926L^3 - 4085L^4)(RM_t - \bar{\Pi}_t)$ $+ (353 + 188L + 94L^2 - 65L^3 + 23L^4) GNP_t]$
8	EUD^c_{2t}	$= (1 - 0.898L - 0.286L^2 - 0.098L^3 + 0.367L^4)^{-1}$ $[-13.1 - 21.4D1_t + 61.1D2_t + 9.7D3_t$ $+ (80 - 684L - 450L^2 + 109L^3 + 76L^4)(R_t - \bar{\Pi}_t)$ $+ (77 + 47L - 54L^2 - 92L^3 + 24L^4) GNP_t]$
9	EUD^c_{3t}	$= (1 - 0.970L + 0.026L^2 - 0.347L^3 + 0.333L^4)^{-1}$ $[-12.0 + 1.1D1_t + 32.2D2_t + 10.4D3_t$ $+ (188 - 211L - 520L^2 + 584L^3 - 14L^4)(R_t - \bar{\Pi}_t)$ $+ (38 + 18L + 39L^2 - 16L^3 + 23L^4) GNP_t]$
10	EUD^c_{4t}	$= (1 - 1.17L - 0.113L^2 + 0.211L^3 + 0.149L^4)^{-1}$ $[1.17 + 2.28D1_t + 1.16D2_t + 0.36D3_t$ $+ (-26 + 10L + 14L^2 - 20L^3 - 28L^4) GNP_t]$
11	EUD^c_{5t}	$= (1 - 0.426L + 0.033L^2 - 0.182L^3 - 0.309L^4)^{-1}$ $[-8.47 - 6.59D1_t + 21.84D2_t + 15.76D3_t$ $+ (33 - 3L + 13L^2 - 7L^3 - 18L^4) GNP_t]$
12	EUD^c_{6t}	$= (1 - 0.806L + 0.255L^2 - 0.156L^3 + 0.092L^4)^{-1}$ $[-7.03 + 8.39D1_t + 18.43D2_t - 10.32D3_t$ $+ (-130 + 77L - 93L^2 + 151L^3 + 34L^4) GNP_t]$
13	EUD^c_{it}	$= EUD_{it} - EUD^r_{it} \qquad i = 1, \ldots, 6$
14	EUD^r_{Lt}	$= \text{cubic spline } (HS^r_{LT}) \qquad L = 1, 2, 3$
15	EUD^r_{4t}	$= 37.4 + 0.90 TREND_t$
16	EUD^r_{5t}	$= 67.7 + 0.89 TREND_t$
17	EUD^r_{6t}	$= 57.4 + 1.6 TREND_t$

Macroeconomic Equations

No.	Dependent Variable	Equation
18	RM_t	$= (1 - 1.06L + 0.477L^2 - 0.449L^3 + 0.078L^4)^{-1}$ $[-0.0001 + (0.080 + 0.079L - 0.055L^2 - 0.003L^3$ $- 0.024L^4)R_t]$
19	G_t	$= (1 - 0.702L - 0.261L^2 + 0.167L^3 + 0.043L^4)^{-1}$ $[0.000 + (-0.991L + 0.409L^2 + 0.305L^3 + 0.155L^4)\ GNP_t$ $+ (-0.93L + 0.650L^2 + 1.46L^3 - 0.406L^4)\Pi_t$ $+ (-0.605L - 0.218L^2 + 0.179L^3 + 0.213L^4)M_t$ $+ (-8.11L + 2.20L^2 + 4.37L^3 + 0.505L^4)\ (R_t - \Pi_t)]$
20	GNP_t	$= (1 - 0.454L - 0.049L^2 + 0.250L^3 - 0.003L^4)^{-1}$ $[0.020 + (0.007L - 0.017L^2 - 0.045L^3 + 0.393L^4)G_t$ $+ (0.557L - 0.002L^2 - 0.509L^3 + 0.152L^4)\Pi_t$ $+ (0.615L - 0.030L^2 - 0.020L^3 + 0.086L^4)M_t$ $+ (-1.64L + 2.72L^2 - 2.62L^3 + 1.04L^4)\ (R_t - \bar{\Pi}_t)]$
21	Π_t	$= (1 - 0.295L - 0.438L^2 - 0.179L^3 + 0.002L^4)^{-1}$ $[0.010 + (0.012L - 0.012L^2 - 0.015L^3 + 0.241L^4)G_t$ $+ (-0.063L - 0.073L^2 - 0.066L^3 - 0.059L^4)\ GNP_t$ $+ (0.104L + 0.132L^2 + 0.064L^3 - 0.009L^4)M_t$ $+ (1.11L - 0.415L^2 - 0.611L^3 + 0.124L^4)\ (R_t - \bar{\Pi}_t)]$
22	M_t	$= (1 + 0.114L + 0.142L^2 + 0.040L^3 - 0.091L^4)^{-1}$ $[0.002 + (0.0111L + 0.095L^2 + 0.090L^3 + 0.022L^4)G_t$ $+ (0.1823L + 0.298L^2 + 0.002L^3 + 0.064L^4)\ GNP_t$ $+ (-0.518L - 0.054L^2 - 0.076L^3 + 0.076L^4)\Pi_t$ $+ (-2.94L + 3.99L^2 - 1.29L^3 + 0.437L^4)\ (R_t - \bar{\Pi}_t)]$
23	$(R_t - \bar{\Pi}_t)$	$= (1 - 1.30L + 0.624L^2 - 0.576L^3 + 0.309L^4)^{-1}$ $[-0.001 + (0.007L - 0.017L^2 + 0.005L^3 + 0.005L^4)G_t$ $+ (0.030L + 0.004L^2 - 0.004L^3 - 0.009L^4)\ GNP_t$ $+ (0.017L - 0.047L^2 + 0.666L^3 - 0.016L^4)\Pi_t$ $+ (0.013L + 0.028L^2 + 0.030L^3 - 0.016L^4)M_t]$
24	$\bar{\Pi}_t$	$= 0.083\ (1 - L - L^2 \ldots - L^{11})\Pi_t$

Housing Start Trend Equations

No.	Dependent Variable	Equation	
25	HS_{LT}^{τ}	$= \Delta OHK_{LT}^{\tau} + \Delta VHK_{LT}^{\tau} + LHK_{LT}^{\tau}$	$L = 1, 2, 3$
26	OHK_{LT}^{τ}	$= ohk_{LT}^{\tau} HH_T^{\tau}$	$L = 1, 2, 3$
27	HH_T^{τ}	$= \sum_m hh_{mT}^{\tau} POP_{mT}$	$m = 1, \ldots, 7$
30	hh_{mT}^{τ}	$= 0.095\delta_m - \beta_m \text{ave (RUC)}$ $+ [1 - 0.905 (1 - 0.905L)^{-1}(1 - L)] (hh_{mT} + \beta_m RUC_t)$ $\delta' = [\delta_1, \ldots, \delta_7] = [0.03, 0.31, 0.29, 0.24, 0.13, 0.11, 0.36]$ $\beta' = [\beta_1, \ldots, \beta_7] = (2, 1, 0.5, 0.25, 0.125, 0.125, 0.25]$	$m = 1, \ldots, 7$
31	ohk_{1T}^{τ}	$= \sum_n \sum_o \omega_{noT}^{\tau} ohk_{1noT}^{\tau}$	$n = 1, 4$ $o = 1, 2, 3$
32	ohk_{2T}^{τ} or HH_T^{τ}	$= (1 - ohk_{1T}^{\tau} - ohk_{3T}^{\tau})$ $= \sum_L OHK_{LT}^{\tau}$	
33	ohk_{3T}^{τ}	$= ohk_{3T-1}^{\tau} + 0.0017 + 0.5 [(1 - L) ohk_{3T} - 0.0017]$	
34	ohk_{1noT}^{τ}	$= ohk_{1noT-1}^{\tau} + \delta_{no}$ $+ 0.5\{[1 - L][ohk_{1noT} + \beta_{no}(RUC_T$ $- \text{ave (RUC)}] - 100\delta_{no}\}$ $\delta' = [\delta_{11}, \delta_{21}, \ldots, \delta_{43}]$ $= - [0.09, 0.28, 0.31, 0.34, 0.39, 0.47, 0.66, 0.67, 0.60, 0.46, 0.88, 0.56]$ $\beta' = [\beta_{11}, \beta_{21}, \ldots, \beta_{43}]$ $= [0.15, 0.36, 0.37, 0.27, 0.40, 0.42, 0.34, 0.40, 0.43, 0.31, 0.38, 0.39]$	$n = 1, 4$ $o = 1, 2, 3$
35	ω_{noT}^{τ}	$= \omega_{noT}$ $= \delta_{no} + 100\beta_{no} TREND_T$ $\delta' = [\delta_{11}, \delta_{21}, \ldots, \delta_{43}]$ $= [0.11, 0.10, 0.05, 0.10, 0.08, 0.11, 0.09, 0.06, 0.14, 0.06, 0.06, 0.03]$ $\beta' = [\beta_{11}, \beta_{21}, \ldots, \beta_{43}]$ $= [-0.13, 0.00, -0.02, -0.11, 0.06, -0.07, -0.02, 0.20, 0.01, 0.01, 0.14, 0.04]$	$T < 1980$ $n = 1, 4$ $o = 1, 2, 3$ $T \geqslant 1980$

Summary Statistics for Estimated Equations

Dependent Variable	R^2	$\hat{\sigma}$	DW	Q	Estimation Period
$\Delta \log(MLC_t)$	0.969	0.0027	2.07	28.11	1968:2–1979:4
Z_t	0.912	0.112	2.00	13.91	1968:2–1979:4
$QRESID_t$	0.738	125.3	2.01	18.98	1968:2–1979:4
EUD^c_{1t}	0.930	19.8	1.85	35.22	1964:1–1979:4
EUD^c_{2t}	0.936	17.5	2.20	17.37	1964:1–1979:4
EUD^c_{3t}	0.947	8.9	2.30	56.5	1964:1–1979:4
EUD^c_{4t}	0.955	4.3	1.96	21.9	1964:1–1979:4
EUD^c_{5t}	0.826	9.9	1.88	12.21	1964:1–1979:4
EUD^c_{6t}	0.584	24.3	2.02	29.75	1964:1–1979:4
RM_t	0.995	0.001	2.01	25.27	1964:1–1979:4
G_t	0.853	0.142	1.99	33.76	1951:1–1979:4
GNP_t	0.548	0.031	2.02	35.91	1951:1–1979:4
Π_t	0.647	0.020	1.94	23.33	1951:1–1979:4
M_t	0.241	0.047	2.03	28.52	1951:1–1979:4
$R_t - \bar{\Pi}_t$	0.908	0.006	2.01	20.53	1951:1–1979:4

R^2: proportion of explained variation; DW: Durbin-Watson statistic; Q: Box-Pierce. q-statistic; $\hat{\sigma}$: standard error of estimate.

Data Set Construction and Sources

EUD_1	Thousands of new, private, single-unit houses started, quarterly 1959:1–1986:2. Single-unit starts were constructed from the CITIBASE non-seasonally adjusted monthly series HS6P1.
EUD_2	Thousands of new, private, multiunit housing units started, quarterly 1959:1–1986:2. Multiunit starts were constructed from the CITIBASE nonseasonally adjusted monthly series HS6FR.
EUD_3	Thousands of new mobile homes shipped, quarterly 1959:1–1986:2. Mobile home shipments were constructed from the CITIBASE non-seasonally adjusted monthly series HMOB6.
EUD_4	Private nonresidential construction expenditures in millions of 1982 dollars, quarterly 1947:1–1986:2. Nonresidential construction expenditures were constructed from the seasonally adjusted CITIBASE monthly series CONR and the GNP deflator.
EUD_5	Expenditures on residential repairs and alterations in millions of 1982 dollars, quarterly 1962:1–1985:4. Repair and alterations expenditures were constructed from the Department of Commerce, Bureau of Census, Expenditures by All Residential Property Owners C-50 nonseasonally adjusted series and the GNP deflator. Missing data for quarters in 1963 were based on linear interpolation of adjoining year averages; the quarterly distribution was adjusted by an estimated multiplicative seasonal index.
EUD_6	Exports of softwood lumber from Oregon and Washington customs districts in millions of board feet, lumber tally, (MMBF, LT), quarterly 1961:1–1986:2. This nonseasonally adjusted series was obtained from U.S. Department of Agriculture, Forest Service (serial).
G	Federal deficit in billions of 1982 dollars, quarterly 1947:1–1986:2. The constant-dollar deficit was constructed as the ratio of the nominal NIPA deficit from the seasonally adjusted CITIBASE series GGFNET to the GNP implicit price deflator.
GNP	Annualized growth rate in real GNP, quarterly 1947:1–1986:2. Real GNP growth was constructed from the seasonally adjusted CITIBASE series GNP82.
hh_m	Fraction of persons in age class m who are heads of households, annually 1952–85. Household headship rates were constructed as $HH_m*(POP20_m/POP25_m)^r$. HH_m is the household headship rate reported in U.S. Department of Commerce, Bureau of the Census, Current Population Survey, Current Population Reports, series P-20. $POP20_m$ is the resident population in age class m as reported in the series P-20 publication "Marital Status & Living Arrangements." $POP25_m$ is the

(Continued)

Data Set Construction and Sources (*Continued*)

	resident noninstitutional population in age class m as reported in the Current Population Reports, series P-25, publication "Population Estimates and Projections." $(POP20_m/POP25_m)^r$ is the trend in the ratio of these series as given by the fitted values of an ordinary least squares (OLS) regression on a linear time trend. Current year reports generally give estimates of March values. Linear interpolation was used to get estimates of year-end values. See Hendershott and Smith (1985) for a discussion of why transformations such as these are necessary. Trend household formations were calculated from products of the POP25 series and the trend in headship rates.
M	Annualized growth rate in the stock of 1982 dollar money balances, quarterly 1947:1–1986:2. The constant-dollar level of the money stock was constructed as the ratio of the nominal stock of M1 from an average of the seasonally adjusted monthly CITIBASE series FM1 to the GNP implicit price deflator.
MLC	Average variable manufacturing and logging cost for coastal lumber mills in current \$/MBF, LT, quarterly 1967:1–1985:2. The quarterly series was interpolated from an annual series by quasicubic spline. The annual series was constructed by applying estimated MLC growth rates to an initial benchmark MLC of \$42 in 1966. Growth rates were obtained from Adams et al. (1979) for 1966–70, the May 1981 issue of the DRI FORSIM Review for 1971–75, and the May 1985 issue of FORSIM Review for 1976–85.
MS_j	Share of new orders originating in census region j that are placed with Coastal Region producers, quarterly 1963:2–1985:2. The quarterly series was interpolated by quasicubic spline from an annual series. For 1972–85 the annual series was provided by Resources Information Systems, Inc., the current operator of the FORSIM service. Market shares for the pre-1972 period were constructed by extrapolating the 1972–85 series backward.
ohk_{1no}	Share of those occupied units in region n, of metropolitan status o, that are single-unit type, annually 1960–79. Data for 1960 and 1970 are from the decennial censuses. Data for 1974–79 are from the *Annual Housing Survey*. Missing data points were constructed by linear interpolation.
Overrun	Factor for converting from the scribner log scale volume denomination to lumber tally, quarterly 1963:3–1985:2. Overrun is a fraction, thousand board feet, log scale, scribner (MBF, LS, S). The quarterly series was interpolated by quasicubic spline from an annual series. For 1963–72 the annual series increases from a base of 1.39 by 0.01 per year. From 1972 onward the series equals those published in the May 1981 and May 1985 issues of FORSIM Review.

Data Set Construction and Sources (*Continued*)

P	Douglas-fir FOB lumber price for coastal mills in current \$/MBF, LT, quarterly 1967:1–1984:2. The series was constructed from monthly price and volume series by grade category as reported in the Western Wood Products Association (serial), "Summary of Past Sales: Coast Key Items." Quarterly price series by grade category were constructed as volume-weighted averages of the monthly price series. In an effort to purge the series of the growing quality differential between USFS logs and logs from all sources, P was constructed as a fixed-weight averages of these clear and common grade price indices with respective weights equaling their 1967:1 volume shares of (0.2, 0.8).
POP_m	Resident noninstitutional population in age class m. This is the Current Population Reports, series P-25, discussed in the documentation of hh_m.
Π	Annualized growth rate in the GNP deflator, quarterly 1947:1–1986:2. The GNP deflator was constructed as the ratio of the two seasonally adjusted CITIBASE series GNP and GNP82.
Q	New orders for lumber from coastal mills in millions of board feet, lumber tally (MMBF, LT), quarterly 1962:1–1986:4. Constructed from the latest revisions of the monthly series in the Western Wood Products Association (serial), "Western Lumber Facts," provided in summary form directly by the WWPA. Since only annual revisions were available for 1976–82, the interquarterly distributions from the unrevised series were used to interpolate the annual revisions for these years.
R	Annualized coupon-equivalent nominal yield on three-month U.S. Treasury bills, quarterly 1947:1–1986:2. The T bill rate was constructed from the CITIBASE monthly discount basis series FYGN3.
R^k	Unit rental cost of capital for coastal lumber mills in current \$/MBF, LT, quarterly 1967:1–1984:2. The quarterly series was interpolated from an annual series by quasicubic spline. The annual rental cost of capital is the product of an estimate of the real capital stock, K, and a nominal rental rate, u. For 1955–79, K was constructed by a perpetual inventory recursion using annual gross plant and equipment expenditures by state at the three-digit standard industrial classification level. For 1980–84, K was extrapolated at the growth rate of single-shift mill capacity, as reported in the Washington Mill survey series. The nominal rental rate, u, is given by $u = q(RP + \delta)/(1 - \tau)$, where q is the acquisition cost of one constant dollar of capital stock as measured by the implicit price deflator for nonresidential investment, RP is the prime interest rate, $\delta = 0.15$ is the capital depreciation rate, and τ is the marginal corporate tax rate. To convert the aggregate rental cost to a unit basis, the $u*K$ series was divided by the total industry production series of Merrifield and Singleton (1986). David Merrifield graciously provided the production, investment, and tax rate data.

(Continued)

Data Set Construction and Sources (*Continued*)

RM	Annualized nominal mortgage rate, quarterly 1963:1–1985:4. The nominal mortgage rate was constructed by averaging the nonseasonally adjusted monthly Federal Home Loan Bank Board Survey series of the effective rate on fixed rate loans for the purchase of previously occupied homes. Mimeographs containing survey results were obtained from the FHLBB.
$RSEUD_{1j}$	Share of national single-unit houses started in census region j, quarterly 1964:1–1986:4. Single-unit shares were constructed from the regional private housing start series in U.S. Department of Commerce, Bureau of the Census, "Housing Starts," Construction Reports C-20.
$RSEUD_{2j}$	Share of national multiunit dwellings started in census region j, quarterly 1964:1–1986:4. See $RSEUD_{1j}$ for source.
$RSEUD_{3j}$	Share of national mobile homes shipped in census region j, quarterly 1964:1–1986:4. The 1974:1–1986:4 values were constructed as the region's share of new mobile homes placed for residential use, as given in the U.S. Department of Commerce, Bureau of the Census, survey on mobile homes. Earlier values were set at the average of the 1974:1–1986:4 values.
$RSEUD_{4j}$	Share of national nonresidential construction expenditures in census region j, quarterly 1964:1–1985:2. The series was constructed as the share of listed value on nonresidential building permits issued, as reported in U.S. Department of Commerce, Bureau of the Census, Construction Review.
$RSEUD_{5j}$	Share of national residential repairs and alterations expenditures in census region j, quarterly 1964:1–1984:4. Interpolated by quasi-cubic spline from an annual series. The annual series was constructed from the regional series on residential repairs and alterations expenditures in the U.S. Department of Commerce, C-50 series, publications.
$RSEUD_{6j}$	Share of softwood lumber exports in census region j. By definition, this share is unity in the rest-of-the-world consumption region and is zero elsewhere.
RUC	The real user cost of owner-occupied housing, expressed as a fraction of the house price, annually 1955–79. The user cost of housing was constructed as the average of the quarterly series in Hendershott and Shilling (1981) for a tax rate of 0.15.
S	Average price of douglas-fir stumpage sold on Westside Region 6 U.S. forests in $/MBF, LT, quarterly 1963:1–1986:1. Constructed from the $/MBF, LS series in U.S. Department of Agriculture, Forest Service (serial).

Data Set Construction and Sources (*Continued*)

UF_{1j}	Softwood lumber used per new single-unit house in Census region j, quarterly 1964:1–1984:2. The quarterly series was interpolated by quasicubic spline from an annual series. For 1962 to 1970 the annual series follows the rates of change given in U.S. Department of Agriculture, Forest Service (1982). For 1970 to 1984, the level of the series equals those reported in the May 1981 and May 1985 issues of FORSIM Review.
UF_{2j}	Softwood lumber used for new multiunit dwelling in census region j, quarterly 1964:1–1984:2. See UF_{1j} for source.
UF_{3j}	Softwood lumber used per new mobile home in census region j, quarterly 1964:1–1984:2. See UF_{1j} for source.
UF_{4j}	Softwood lumber used per constant 1982 dollar spent on nonresidential construction in census region j, quarterly 1964:1–1984:2. The quarterly series was interpolated by quasicubic spline from an annual series. The annual series was based on a FORSIM series; see UF_{1j} for source. Because FORSIM uses a different measure of nonresidential construction expenditures than does EUD_4, the use factor was scaled by the average ratio of the FORSIM nonresidential construction series to EUD_4.
UF_{5j}	Softwood lumber used per constant 1982 dollar spent on residential repairs and alterations in census region j, quarterly 1964:1–1984:2. The source and method of data construction for this series are the same as for UF_{4j}.
UF_{6j}	Softwood lumber used per export of softwood lumber, unity by definition.
ω_{no}	Share of the nation's households that are in region n with metropolitan status o, annually 1960–79. See ohk_{1no} for source.

Additional Exogenous Variables

D1	Dummy variable equaling 1 in the first quarter
D2	First lag of D1
D3	Second lag of D1
LHK_L^i	Trend flow of net losses to the housing stock, by type of unit L. As explained in Mattey (1988), this variable was constructed from an analysis of data on the components of housing inventory change from the decennial Census of Housing and the Annual Housing Survey (AHS).
TREND	Time trend increasing by 1 each quarter, 1949:1 = 1.
VHK_L^i	Trend level of vacant housing units, by type of unit L. As explained in Mattey (1988), this variable was constructed from an analysis of frictional and nonfrictional housing vacancies. Annual series on owner and rental vacancy rates for 1956–85 were obtained from U.S. Department of Commerce, Bureau of the Census, Current Housing Reports, "Housing Vacancies," series H-111. Nonfrictional vacancy data were obtained from the decennial Census of Housing and the Annual Housing Survey (AHS)

Notes

Chapter 1

1. This book focuses on the market for coastal USFS timber. Only some of the description and analysis it contains would apply to timber sales in other regions or by other agencies.

2. See U.S. Congress (1984).

3. See the statement of Mark Rey (U.S. House of Representatives, 1989a, pp. 325–26).

4. I computed these statistics on the buyout from records on individual firms provided by Region 6, the Regional Forester's Buyout Determination Summary.

5. See Mead, Schniepp, and Watson (1981, 1983) and Rucker (1984) for alternative studies of timber price determination in this period.

Chapter 2

1. U.S. Senate, (1982), p. 14.

2. U.S. Senate, (1983), pp. 359–60.

3. FORSIM Review, February 1982, p. 13.

4. Ibid.

5. The problems with monetary control include the impact of changes in the menu of financial instruments on the interpretation of conventional monetary aggregates and the impact of lagged reserve accounting on the Federal Reserve's ability to control total reserves. See, for example, Hester (1981) and Pierce (1981).

6. Council of Economic Advisers, (1986), p. 36.

7. See, for example, Adams, Duggal, and Thanwala (1976).

8. The distinction between industry shipments and industry orders is important for short time horizons. This book ignores the distinction because

the model is used to predict industry quantity flows at the end of a three-year horizon.

9. Unlike some other industrial-linkage models, this model does not exclusively use the Bureau of Economic Analysis's National Income and Product Account (NIPA) measures of final demand. NIPA measures of final demand are presented on a current-dollar or a constant-dollar expenditure basis, not on a physical quantity basis. For a commodity such as lumber, it is easier to translate final demands that are measured in physical quantities into lumber volumes.

10. According to the May 1985 issue of the FORSIM Review, for 1978 each million units of multiunit starts in the West created 5.7 billion board feet of softwood lumber demand, but a million units in the Northeast created only 2.8 billion board feet of softwood lumber demand.

11. FORSIM estimates of market share are used. Estimates of coastal market share can be constructed from regional lumber shipments data published by industry statistical services such as the Western Wood Products Association. The FORSIM estimates of market share are favored over the direct translation of industry shipments data because the industry shipments data indicate only the original destination of the shipments, whereas the FORSIM estimates incorporate subjective adjustments for trans-shipments. Trans-shipment is the practice of using an intermediate destination to obtain more favorable freight rates.

12. Following the Merrifield and Singleton (1986) research on the dynamic conditional factor demand schedules of the Washington and Oregon lumber industry, the index of capital costs is constructed as a rental cost in the sense of Hall and Jorgenson (1967). See Mattey (1988) for details on construction of the capital cost index. David Merrifield graciously provided some of the data needed to construct the capital cost index.

13. No particular signs were anticipated for the innovations in the equations for macroeconomic variables; note that these innovations are not orthogonalized.

14. There were other large swings in orders for coastal lumber in the 1960s and 1970s. For example, after rising to a peak of 9.2 BBF in 1972, lumber orders fell 20 percent to a trough of 7.4 BBF in 1974.

15. Note that in this type of decomposition the sum of explained variation can exceed 100 percent.

16. Actually, the system is linear in deflated timber values. The current dollar timber value projection is calculated as the product of a projection of deflated timber values and a projection of manufacturing and logging costs.

17. See Mattey (1988).

18. The Monte Carlo experiments draw from a Wishart distribution for the variance–covariance matrix of the error terms of the system and from a

normal distribution, given the variance–covariance, for the coefficients on regressors. See Mattey (1988) for a full description of the method.

19. Mankiw, Miron, and Weil (1987), p. 371.

20. Ibid.

Chapter 3

1. The following exposition of the bankruptcy model is based on the Golbe (1988) representation.

2. See Lockhart, Long, and Sefcik (1987) for a description of some of the creative accounting techniques that the regulators promulgated to create a façade that capital adequacy standards were being enforced.

3. The chairman of the Federal Home Loan Bank Board (Gray, 1986, p. 1) noted quite a while ago that delaying the resolution of insolvent thrift cases would ultimately raise the costs to the Federal Savings and Loan Insurance Corporation. Those who have attributed these increased costs specifically to zombie effects include Benston and Kaufman (1985); Barth, Brumbaugh, Sauerhaft, and Wang (1985); Barth, Brumbaugh, and Sauerhaft (1986); and Brumbaugh and Carron (1987). Golbe (1988) and Kendall (1988) have provided theoretical support for the notion that firms facing imminent closure have the incentive to take more risks.

4. The U.S. Department of Agriculture (1985) indicated that over 1978–80, USFS timber contract prices rose only 15 percent in the South and 25 percent in the Pacific Southwest, but douglas-fir prices rose 73 percent in the Coastal Pacific Northwest. Some, but not all, of the differential rates of bid appreciation can be explained by the existence of stumpage rate adjustment clauses (partial indexation of timber prices paid to product price movements) in regions other than the Coastal.

5. Statement of John B. Crowell, Jr., Assistant Secretary for Natural Resources and the Environment, USDA (U.S. Senate, 1982, pp. 288–89).

6. Statement of John Davis of Williamette Industries (U.S. Senate, 1982, p. 90).

7. Statement of James Geisinger (U.S. Senate, 1983, p. 418). Geisinger also recounted that in January 1983, when the mill started up again, the event got so much attention that CBS "Nightly News" sent a crew to Sheridan, Oregon, in limousines larger than any cars the community had ever seen. When Senator Metzenbaum facetiously inquired if this event helped the local economy, Geisinger replied that he did not know whether they bought any gasoline.

8. Statement of James F. Stock of the Clear Lumber Company (U.S. Senate, 1982, p. 191).

9. U.S. Senate (1982), pp. 413–14.

10. U.S. Senate (1983), p. 170.

11. This statement of purpose and the following description of the SBA set-aside program are based on the General Accounting Office (1979) publication on the set-aside program.

12. The recomputed base share was set equal to the small firms' actual share over the preceding five-year period.

13. See General Accounting Office (1979), p. 38.

14. Statement of Edward Hines (U.S. Senate, 1983, p. 497).

15. Statement of Forrest H. Dobson (U.S. Senate, 1982, p. 153). The Chelan marketing area is in an Eastside Region 6 forest.

16. Statement of Fred Sohn (U.S. Senate, 1982, p. 78).

17. Statement of Anna Bevens (U.S. Senate, 1983, p. 421).

18. Statement of C. Donald Fisher (U.S. Senate, 1983, p. 194).

19. See Schuldt and Howard (1974) and the 1981 issue of State of Washington, *Washington Mill Survey Series*, for lists of the counties in the six subregions.

20. Observed rates of disinvestment in the six subregions over 1976–82 were 0.109, − 0.030, 0.161, 0.186, 0.274, 0.156, respectively. These figures are the rates of decrease in installed single-shift capacity of lumber mills, as calculated from tables in State of Washington, *Washington Mill Survey Series*; Howard and Hiserote (1978); and Howard (1984). Capacity data were obtained from these sources; from Manock, Choate, and Gedney (1971); and from Schuldt and Howard (1974).

21. The average fraction of lumber mills more than one-third dependent on USFS logs in 1968, 1972, and 1976 was 0.184, 0.185, 0.267, 0.271, 0.531, 0.415 in the six subregions, respectively. The proxy for planned disinvestment by subregion is − 2.2, − 2.2, − 0.7, − 0.7, 4.0, 1.9, in percentage points. For example, the proxy indicates that the planned rate of disinvestment in West Central Oregon was 4.0 percentage points higher than the average rate of planned disinvestment across all six regions.

22. A second-order autoregression in new lumber orders and the change in timber conversion values was used to form the expectations proxies. The volume-weighted average of the statistical high bids on douglas-fir, western hemlock, and white-fir species was used as the bid price. A douglas-fir, hem-fir lumber price series was used in calculating timber conversion values.

23. These appraised net rates are for the douglas-fir, hem-fir species.

24. The quality variable does not fully capture the different characteristics of salvage sales because the appraisals use historic prices to calculate revenue estimates. The size of the discrepancy between revenue estimates using historic prices and revenue estimates using expected future prices is likely to be different across salvage sales and nonsalvage sales.

25. The discussion proceeds as if timber buyers expected to use bankruptcy protection to limit liabilities. The general point is that anticipation of the ability to truncate losses probably contributed to the overbidding. For the most part, congressional modification of timber contracts, not bankruptcy, actually was used to truncate losses.

Chapter 4

1. This use of the term "quasirationality" follows Russell and Thaler (1985).

2. Statement of A. A. Emmerson (U.S. Senate, 1982, p. 134).

3. Statement of Barbara Webb (U.S. Senate, 1983, p. 73).

4. Statement of M. J. Kuehne (U.S. Senate, 1982, p. 377).

5. Statement of Lynn Newbry (U.S. Senate, 1982, pp. 86–87).

6. Ibid, pp. 23–24.

7. See National Forest Products Association (1980).

8. This is not a compound rate.

9. Statement of John Davis (U.S. Senate, 1982, p. 90).

10. Statement of John J. Stephens (U.S. Senate, 1982, p. 428).

11. The USFS included vacant units recently sold or rented, not just units for sale and for rent, in frictional vacancies.

12. See the appendix and Mattey (1988) for details on the specification of the baseline trend in housing starts.

13. The housing start and household formation data cited here are annualized averages over 1980:1–80:3 of the housing start and household variables described in the data appendix. The figure on additional vacant units was derived by applying the vacancy rates in the 1979 and 1983 issues of the *Annual Housing Survey* (AHS) to housing unit totals that were benchmarked to the 1980 Census results; that is, 1.8 million units were added to the count of housing units originally reported in the 1979 AHS. The net loss figure was derived from the housing start, household formation, and vacant unit change data via the inventory identity.

14. TAMM's lumber supply equation for the Coastal Region was estimated by two-stage least squares (2SLS) on 1951–76 annual data and yielded the following fitted relationship:

$$Q_t = 4019.8 + 22.90(P_t - \text{MLC}_t - S_t) + 0.527Q_{t-1}$$

The equation is a regression of lumber production Q on its previous quarter level, average douglas-fir mill price in the coastal region P, USFS indices of prices for douglas-fir stumpage cut S, and average variable manufacturing and logging costs MLC. Each of the nominal variables was deflated by the all-commodities PPI. The full-adjustment elasticity is 0.44 at the sample means of the data.

15. Haynes and Adams (1985), p. 53.

16. The revised version of TAMM used in the 1983 timber assessment update also has a biased estimate of coastal lumber supply elasticity. The Haynes and Adams (1985) estimates of coastal lumber supply elasticity are grossly inaccurate because the regional supply equations were estimated jointly under the constraint of equal coefficients on margins in all regions. While a constraint of equal elasticities in all regions is plausible, the constraint that the coefficients on margins are equal is not plausible. Mean output in the Coastal Region substantially exceeds that in each other TAMM production region, but the price levels are the same order of magnitude in all regions. Thus under the assumption that elasticities are equal across regions, the constraint of equal coefficients on margins introduces a significant downward bias in the estimator of coastal supply elasticity.

17. For example, if the true variable cost of timber differs from the observed cut price by an unpredictable measurement error term, then the coefficient on the margin variable in a lumber supply equation is biased downward.

18. Statement of Arnold Ewing (U.S. Senate, 1982, p. 206).

19. Statement of Fred Sohn (U.S. Senate, 1982, p. 73).

20. Statement of James Geisinger (U.S. Senate, 1983, p. 418).

21. See Johnson (1985) for a fuller discussion of how the Forest Service holds the industry hostage in a battle for a larger budget.

Chapter 5

1. U.S. Department of Agriculture, (1989a), p. 11–1.

2. Ibid.

3. Ibid, p. 6–3.

4. Ibid, p. 11–1.

5. See, for example, Haynes and Adams (1985).

6. 36 Code of Federal Regulations 219, subpart A, July 1, 1988, edition.

7. The forest supervisor is authorized to change forest plan implementation schedules to reflect differences between proposed annual budgets and appropriated funds at 36 Code of Federal Regulations 219, subpart 10e, July 1, 1988, edition.

8. 36 Code of Federal Regulations 219, subpart 16, July 1, 1988, edition.

9. U.S. House of Representatives (1989b), p. 70.

10. Table E.11 of USDA, (1989b).

11. 36 Code of Federal Regulations 221, subpart 3, July 1, 1988, edition.

12. See Dowdle and Johnson (1988) for a related proposal.

13. Final rule published in the Federal Register, Vol. 53, No. 168, for Tuesday, August 30, 1988, to be codified at 36 Code of Federal Regulations 223.

14. Federal Register, Vol. 53, No. 168, Tuesday, August 30, 1988, to be codified at 36 Code of Federal Regulations Part 223.101.

15. Forest Service Handbook 6509.18, Financial Analysis Handbook, draft July 3, 1989.

16. Federal Register, Vol. 50, No. 114, 24788, June 13, 1985.

17. Federal Register, Vol. 50, No. 114, 24789, June 13, 1985.

18. See, for example, U.S. Senate (1988a, 1988b).

19. See, for example, the statement of the North West Timber Association (U.S. Senate, 1988a, p. 89).

20. See Schniepp (1985) for an example of a discussion that presumes the impact of the set-aside program on federal revenues is a key issue.

21. Statement of Monika Edwards Harrison, Associate Administrator for Procurement Assistance of the SBA (U.S. Senate, 1988b, p. 16).

22. Statement of Richard G. Bennett (U.S. Senate, 1988b, pp. 81–82).

23. Statement of R. Dennis Hayward (U.S. Senate, 1988b, p. 45).

24. See 13 Code of Federal Regulations 124.110 (January 1, 1988, edition, p. 403) for a description of the fixed program participation term feature of the SBA program for minority firms.

References

Adams, Darius M., and Richard W. Haynes (1980). "The Softwood Timber Assessment Market Model: Structure, Projections and Policy Simulations." *Forest Science Monograph*, no. 22.

Adams, Darius M., Richard W. Haynes, Thomas J. Mills, David Shearer, and Steven Childress (1979). "Production, Consumption, and Prices of Softwood Products in North America—Regional Time Series Data, 1950–76." *Research Bulletin*, no. 27. Forest Research Laboratory, Oregon State University, Corvallis.

Adams, F. Gerard, Vijaya Duggal, and Sheila Thanwala (1976, September). "Industrial Linking Functions for the Macro Models." *Business Economics*, 87–90.

Barth, James R., R. Dan Brumbaugh, and Daniel Sauerhaft (1986). "The Thrift Industry's Rough Road Ahead." *Challenge*, **29**, 38–43.

Barth, James R., R. Dan Brumbaugh, Daniel Sauerhaft, and George Wong (1985). "Thrift-Institution Failures: Causes and Policy Issues." In *Bank Structure and Competition*. Chicago: Federal Reserve Bank of Chicago, pp. 217–50.

Benston, George J., and George G. Kaufman (1985, December). "Risks and Failures in Banking: Overview, History, and Evaluation." Mimeo.

Blanchard, Olivier J. (1984). "The Lucas Critique and the Volcker Deflation." *AER Papers & Proceedings*, **74**(2), 211–15.

Brumbaugh, R. Dan, and Andrew S. Carron (1987). "Thrift Industry Crisis: Causes and Solutions." *Brookings Papers on Economic Activity*, **2**, 349–87.

Bulow, Jeremy, and John Shoven (1978). "The Bankruptcy Decision." *Bell Journal of Economics*, **7**, 437–56.

Cardellichio, Peter A., and Johan Veltkamp (1981). "Demand for Pacific Northwest Timber and Timber Products." *Forest Policy Project, Study Module II-A*, Pacific Northwest Regional Commission.

CITIBASE: Citibank economic database [machine-readable magnetic data file] 1946–. New York: Citibank, N.A.

Council of Economic Advisers (1986). "The Annual Report of the Council of Economic Advisers." In *Economic Report of the President*. Washington, D.C.: Government Printing Office.

Craig, George A. (1982). "The Lumber Depression and Other Considerations Justifying Relief from Forest Service Contracts." As reproduced in U.S. Senate (1983), pp. 341–58.

Dowdle, Barney, and M. Bruce Johnson (1988, July). "Marketable Rights for Public Timber: Reducing Regulatory Inefficiencies." Paper presented at the meeting of the Western Economic Association, Los Angeles.

Ellefson, Paul V., and Robert N. Stone (1984). *U.S. Wood-Based Industry*. New York: Praeger.

FORSIM Review (serial). Lexington, Mass.: McGraw-Hill for Data Resources, Inc.

General Accounting Office (1979). *Allegations Regarding the Small Business Set-Aside Program for Federal Timber Sales*. Washington, D.C.: Government Printing Office.

Golbe, Devra L. (1988). "Risk-taking by Firms near Bankruptcy." *Economics Letters*, **28**, 75–90.

Gray, Edwin J. (1986, March 13). "Statement Before the Committee on Banking, Housing, and Urban Affairs, U.S. Senate." Mimeo.

Hall, Robert E., and Dale W. Jorgenson (1967). "Tax Policy and Investment Behavior." *American Economic Review*, **57**, 391–414.

Hampton, John C., and Carol A. Wood (1982). "Federal Timber Contracts: Who Will Bear the Ultimate Costs if Congress Denies Modifications?" *Williamette Law Review*, **19**(2), as reproduced in U.S. Senate (1983), pp. 102–25.

Haynes, Richard W., and Darius M. Adams (1985). *Simulations of the Effects of Alternative Assumptions on Demand-Supply Determinants on the Timber Situation in the United States*. U.S. Department of Agriculture, Forest Resources Economic Research Publication.

Hendershott, Patric H., and James D. Shilling (1981). "The Economics of Tenure Choice, 1955–1979." In C. F. Sirmans (Ed.), *Research in Real Estate*, vol. 1. Greenwich, Conn.: JAI Press, pp. 105–33.

Hendershott, Patric H., and Mark Smith (1985). "Household Formations." In Patric Hendershott (Ed.), *The Level and Composition of Household Saving*. Cambridge, Mass.: Ballinger.

Hester, Donald (1981). "Innovations and Monetary Control." *Bookings Papers on Economic Activity*, **1**, 141–89.

Howard, James O. (1984). "Oregon's Forest Products Industry: 1982." *Resource Bulletin PNW-118*, U.S. Department of Agriculture, Forest Service, PNW Forest & Range Experiment Station.

Howard, James O., and Bruce A. Hiserote (1978). "Oregon's Forest Products Industry: 1976." *Resource Bulletin PNW-79*, U.S. Department of Agriculture, Forest Service, PNW Forest & Range Experiment Station.

Johnson, Ronald N. (1985). "U.S. Forest Service Policy and Its Budget." In Robert T. Deacon and M. Bruce Johnson, (Eds.), *Forestlands Public and Private*. San Francisco: Pacific Institute for Public Policy Research, pp. 103–33.

Kendall, Sarah B. (1988). "Risk-Taking Incentives in a Regulatory Environment: A Markov Decision Process Model of Bank Portfolio Choice." *OPER Research Paper*, no. 134, Federal Home Loan Bank Board.

Lockhart, Julie A., M. S. Long, and S. E. Sefcik (1987). "Regulatory Accounting Principles, Forbearance, and the Perpetuation of the Savings and Loan Industry." *Housing Finance Review*, 6, 79–91.

Mankiw, N. Gregory, Jeffrey Miron, and David Weil (1987). "The Adjustment of Expectations to a Change in Regime: A Study of the Founding of the Federal Reserve." *American Economic Review*, 77(3), 358–74.

Manock, Eugene R., Grover Choate, and Donald Gedney (1971). *Oregon Timber Industries 1968*. State of Oregon, Department of Forestry.

Mattey, Joe (1988). "Timber and the Macroeconomy: Forward Price Determination in the Presence of Business Cycle Risk." Ph.D. diss., University of California, Berkeley.

Mead, Walter J., Mark Schniepp, and Richard Watson (1981). *The Effectiveness of Competition and Appraisals in the Auction Markets for National Forest Timber in the Pacific Northwest*. U.S. Department of Agriculture, Forest Service.

———(1983). *Competitive Bidding for U.S. Forest Service Timber in the Pacific Northwest, 1963–1983*. U.S. Department of Agriculture, Forest Service.

Merrifield, David E., and William R. Singleton (1986). "A Dynamic Cost and Factor Demand Analysis for the Pacific Northwest Lumber and Plywood Industries." *Forest Science*, 32(1), 220–33.

Muraoka, Dennis D., and Richard B. Watson (1985). "Economic Issues in Federal Timber Sales Procedures." In Robert T. Deacon and M. Bruce Johnson, (Eds.), *Forestlands Public and Private*. San Francisco: Pacific Institute for Public Policy Research, pp. 201–23.

———(1986). "Improving the Efficiency of Federal Timber Sale Procedures: An Update." *Natural Resources Journal*, 26(1), 69–76.

National Forest Products Association (1980). *Wood Supply Goals for U.S. Consumers*. Pamphlet.

O'Laughlin, Jay, and Paul V. Ellefson (1982, December). "Strategies for Corporate Timberland Ownership and Management." *Journal of Forestry*.

Pierce, James (1981, November). "How Regulations Affect Monetary Control." *Journal of Money, Credit, and Banking*, pp. 775–87.

Rucker, Randy (1984). "An Economic Analysis of Bidding and Cutting Behavior on Public Timber Sales Contracts." Ph.D. diss., University of Washington, Seattle.

Rucker, Randy, and Keith Leffler (1986). "To Harvest or Not to Harvest? An Analysis of Cutting Behavior on Federal Timber Sales Contracts." Manuscript, University of Washington, Seattle.

Russell, Thomas, and Richard Thaler (1985). "The Relevance of Quasi Rationality in Competitive Markets." *American Economic Review*, **75**(5), 1071–82.

Schniepp, Mark (1985). "The Economic Consequences of the Setaside Program in the Douglas Fir Region of the Pacific Northwest." In Robert T. Deacon and M. Bruce Johnson, (Eds.), *Forestlands Public and Private*. San Francisco: Pacific Institute for Public Policy Research, pp. 225–45.

Schuldt, John P., and James O. Howard (1974). *Oregon Forest Industries: 1972*. Oregon State University Extension Service publication of joint study with U.S. Forest Service, Forest & Range Experiment Station.

State of Washington (serial). *Washington Mill Survey Series*. Department of Natural Resources, 1968–84.

U.S. Congress (1984). 98 Stat. 2213; *Federal Timber Contract Payment Modification Act*. Public Law no. 98–478.

U.S. Department of Agriculture, Forest Service (serial). *Production, Prices, Employment, and Trade in Northwest Forest Industries*. PNW Forest & Range Experiment Station.

———(1982). *An Analysis of the Timber Situation in the United States 1952–2030*. Forest Resource Report, no. 23.

———(1985). *U.S. Timber Production, Trade, Consumption, and Price Statistics 1950–84*. Miscellaneous Publication, no. 1450.

———(1989a). "An Analysis of the Timber Situation in the United States: 1989–2040. Part II: The Future Resource Situation." Review draft.

———(1989b). *Draft 1990 RPA Program*.

U.S. House of Representatives (1989a). *Timber Sales on National Forests*. Washington, D.C.: Government Printing Office.

———(1989b). *Review of Management of Old-Growth Forests of the Pacific Northwest*. Washington, D.C.: Government Printing Office.

U.S. Senate (1982). *Adjustments to Timber Sale Contracts on National Forest System Lands and Public Lands*. Washington, D.C.: Government Printing Office.

———(1983). *Contracts for the Sale of Federal Timber*. Washington, D.C.: Government Printing Office.

———(1988). *A New Proposal by the Forest Service to Govern Administration of the Small Business Timber Sale Set-Aside Program*. Washington, D.C.: Government Printing Office.

Index